COOL WAR

Noah Feldman

RANDOM HOUSE   NEW YORK

COOL

The Future of Global Competition

WAR

Published in the United States by Random House, an imprint of
The Random House Publishing Group, a division of
Random House, Inc., New York.

RANDOM HOUSE and colophon are registered trademarks
of Random House, Inc.

LIBRARY OF CONGRESS CATALOGING-IN-PUBLICATION DATA

Feldman, Noah
Cool war : the future of global competition / Noah Feldman.
pages   cm
Includes bibliographical references and index.
ISBN 978-0-8129-9274-8
eBook ISBN 978-0-679-64383-8

1. United States—Foreign relations—China. 2. China—Foreign relations—
United States. 3. China—Foreign economic relations—United States. 4. United States—
Foreign economic relations—China. I. Title.
JZ1480.A57F45 2013
327.73051—dc23   2013007907

Printed in the United States of America on acid-free paper

www.atrandom.com

246897531

FIRST EDITION

Book design by Carole Lowenstein

To Penny and Roy Feldman

CONTENTS

Are we on the brink of a new Cold War? The United States is the sole reigning superpower, but it is being challenged by the rising power of China, much as ancient Rome was challenged by Carthage and Britain was challenged by Germany in the years before World War I. Should we therefore think of the United States and China as we once did about the United States and the Soviet Union, two gladiators doomed to an increasingly globalized combat until one side fades?

Or are we entering a new period of diversified global economic cooperation in which the very idea of old-fashioned, imperial power politics has become obsolete? Should we see the United States and China as more like France and Germany after World War II, adversaries wise enough to draw together in an increasingly close circle of cooperation that subsumes neighbors and substitutes economic exchange for geopolitical confrontation?

This is the central global question of our as-yet-unnamed historical moment. What will happen now that America's post–Cold War engagements in Iraq and Afghanistan have run their course and U.S. attention has pivoted to Asia? Can the United States continue to engage China while somehow hedging against the strategic threat it poses? Can China go on seeing the United States both as an object of emulation and also as a barrier to its rightful place on the world stage?

The answer is a paradox: the paradox of cool war.

The term *cool war* aims to capture two different, mutually contradictory historical developments that are taking place simultaneously. A classic struggle for power is unfolding at the same time as economic cooperation is becoming deeper and more fundamental.

The current situation differs from global power struggles of the past. The world's major power and its leading challenger are economically interdependent to an unprecedented degree. China needs the United States to continue buying its products. The United States needs China to continue lending it money. Their economic fates are, for the foreseeable future, tied together. Recognizing the overlapping combination of geostrategic conflict and economic interdependence is the key to making sense of what is coming and what options we have to affect it.

This book grows out of work I did in the first decade of the twenty-first century on the opposition and synthesis of Islam and democracy. My hope then was that a nuanced understanding of the interplay between these ideas and systems might help us rethink the prevalent picture of civilizational conflict. In this second decade of the still-young century, the great issues of conflict and cooperation have shifted. Now U.S. leadership and Western democracy are juxtaposed with China's global aspirations and its protean, emergent governing system. As before, my goal is to add complexity to the dominant conventional accounts.

The stakes of this debate could not possibly be higher. One side argues that the United States must either accept decline or prepare for war. Only by military strength can the United States convince China that it is not worth challenging its status as the sole superpower. Projecting weakness would lead to instability and make war all the more likely.

The other side counters that trying to contain China is the worst thing the United States can do. Excessive defense spending will make the United States less competitive economically. Worse, it will encourage China to become aggressive itself, leading to an arms race that neither side wants and that would itself increase the chances of violence. Much better to engage China politically and economically and encourage it to share the burdens of superpower status.

What we need, I believe, is to change the way we think and talk about the U.S.-China relationship—to develop an alternative to simple images of inevitable conflict or utopian cooperation. We need a way to understand the new structure that draws on historical precedent while recognizing how things are different this time. We need to understand where the United States and China can see eye to eye, and where they cannot compromise. Most of all, we need a way forward to help avoid the real dangers that lie ahead.[1]

This book offers a diagnosis of our situation; an analysis of the ideas and incentives of China's leadership; and an account of how nations, corporations, and peace-seeking institutions are likely to react to a changing world order.[2]

In the first part of the book, I show how the interests of the United States and China often overlap in the realms of trade and economics yet still diverge dramatically when it comes to geopolitical power and ideology. This situation of simultaneous cooperation and conflict needs a new name—cool war—to capture its distinctive features.

In the book's second part, I offer an interpretation of China's leadership. It is not possible to understand the dynamics of a cool war unless we have a more sophisticated understanding of the Chinese Communist Party. No longer ideologically communist, the leadership is pragmatic and committed to preserving its position of power. It seeks to maintain legitimacy through continued growth, regular transitions, and a tentative form of public accountability. It aims to manage deep internal divisions between entitled princelings and self-made meritocrats via a hybrid system that makes room for both types of elites.

Finally, in the third part of the book, I consider the consequences of the emerging cool war. I evaluate the significance of the new situation for countries around the world, for institutions that exist to keep the peace through international cooperation, for multinational corporations that operate everywhere—and for the future of human rights.

The results matter. The complicated interaction between the United States and China will shape war and peace globally and reveal whether the dream of peaceful international cooperation—embodied, albeit shakily, in the European Union—can be extended to countries with less in common. It will determine the future of democracy as a global movement, structure the international strategies of growing powers like India and Brazil, and guide the movements of companies and capital. It will influence the United Nations, the future of international law, and the progress or regress of human rights. Ultimately, like the Cold War before it, this new kind of international engagement will involve every country on earth.

Wherever possible, I have avoided speaking of the American people as "us" or "we." The ideas here should be of use in China, in the West, and elsewhere. The risk of conflict—whether triggered by leaders' mutual misunderstanding or by accurate judgments of diverging interests—must be taken seriously.[3] Reducing the grave dangers of global conflict would serve the United States but also China and the world more generally. The purpose of this book is to start figuring out how we can do so, before it is too late.

PART ONE

COOL WAR

CHAPTER ONE

BOUND TOGETHER

Who won the Cold War?

For twenty years now—almost half the length of the war itself—the Western democracies have assumed that they did. For the first decade after the collapse of the Soviet Union, the United States and Europe grew vastly in the absence of their greatest strategic challenger. The United States generated the information revolution. Europe increased mutual cooperation, united its currency, and incorporated the choicest bits of the former Soviet empire into the European Union. There was good historical precedent for both growth and unity: after the defeat of Napoleon at Waterloo, Britain, the main winner, initiated the industrial revolution, and the Concert of Europe represented the efforts of the European states to cooperate and manage their security affairs.[1]

But in the second decade after the Cold War, two surprising things happened. First, the United States, with European participation, invaded Afghanistan and Iraq and then spent trillions of dollars, enormous diplomatic capital, and thousands of its soldiers' lives in the effort to build functioning states in each. The results were a very partial success in one case and something very much like failure in the other. The economic downturn that began toward the end of the decade was not caused by these misadventures, but taken together they signaled the possibility of imperial decline.[2]

At the same time, China, which had been a secondary player in the Cold War, deepened the experiment it had already begun with state-managed market reform. The result was sustained economic growth of stunning proportions. China became the world's second-largest economy, outstripping Japan and all individual members of the European Union. The pace of its growth has declined from the consistent 10 percent or more of the post–Cold War era to something more like 7.5 percent in 2012, and further slowing remains possible.[3] Yet China weathered the global financial crisis much better than the United States and Europe. Serious observers believe that the Chinese economy could become the biggest in the world in a decade—or even sooner.[4]

Suddenly, the assumption of Western, democratic victory in the Cold War has had to be reexamined. On the level of ideas, capitalism indeed won a significant victory. The communist ideal of a totally nonmarket economy no longer has many adherents outside North Korea and perhaps Cuba. The Communist Party of China has formally welcomed capitalists—defined to include owners of private businesses—into party membership. The Chinese state still owns huge enterprises and guides the economy by controlling banks and by regulating some industries, but the basic theory on which it acts is market capitalism, not communism or even socialism.[5]

Democracy, however, has not won in the way its promoters had hoped.[6] China's ruling elite rejects both elections and individual rights, and it has been able to achieve fast growth and de facto legitimacy without either. After a largely unsuccessful experiment with democracy, Russia has reverted to the rule of a strongman. Much of its public seems to accept, even embrace, this result, notwithstanding some protest. The U.S. experiments with democratic nation building in Afghanistan and Iraq went poorly, not because of any inherent problem with Islam but because of the extreme difficulty of establishing democracy without a strong, functioning state to keep order. Mass demonstrations demanding the end of autocracy deposed dictators in Tunisia and Egypt, yet the Arab Spring has struggled.

Meanwhile, the position of the United States looks much weaker than it should if the Cold War was a definitive victory. The Pax Britannica lasted from 1815 to 1914 before the rise of Germany brought the century of British dominance to an agonizing end. By contrast, in 2013, the rise of China was making the U.S. position as the sole global superpower look tenuous. The United States has arguably been overstretching itself as Britain did over the nineteenth century.[7] The hard fact is that alongside China's extraordinary growth, the U.S. economy has been growing slowly if at all—to the point where 2 percent annual growth would have been considered a victory in 2012.

China's rise—and the relative decline of the United States—sets the stage for the possibility that the real winner of the Cold War could turn out to have been China. Unlike Mikhail Gorbachev, Deng Xiaoping rejected glasnost and insisted on maintaining party rule.[8] And unlike the Soviet Union, China abandoned communist ideology in time to avoid collapse. The emergent party-directed capitalist state is now poised to take its place as a global superpower comparable to the United States.

Interdependence

Yet a powerful argument can be mounted that despite its economic rise, China will not try to challenge the position of the United States as the preeminent global leader. The argument begins with the fact that China's spectacular growth did not take place in isolation. To the contrary, China achieved much of it through export to the United States and other consumer economies. Today trade accounts for half of China's GDP, with exports significantly outstripping imports. The United States alone accounts for roughly 25 percent of Chinese sales.[9] Total trade between the countries amounts to a stunning $500 billion a year.[10]

U.S.-China economic ties go beyond the sale of goods. The United States, a debtor nation, depends on China as the largest purchaser of its bonds. The government of China holds some $1.2 trillion worth of U.S. Treasury debt, or 8 percent of the outstanding total. Only the Federal Reserve and the Social Security Trust Fund, both arms of the government, hold more; all U.S. households combined hold less.[11]

This profound degree of economic interdependence reflects the geostrategic realities of the post–Cold War world, in which the United States largely took responsibility for assuring global stability and open seas. Against the backdrop of a world safe enough for trade, China and the United States began to engage each other on broader and broader scales. Today they and their citizens cooperate not only in the international system but across a wide and repeated range of economic and cultural interactions.

As of the most recent count, 194,000 Chinese students attend U.S. universities and succeed at all levels, from basic undergraduate education to the most advanced graduate students and postdoctoral fellows, especially in science, technology, engineering, and mathematics.[12] Some 70,000 Americans live and study and work in mainland China.[13] U.S.-based architects have taken advantage of China's building boom and now design thousands of remarkable buildings in China that could not be built anywhere else in current economic conditions. American and Chinese businesses invest in each other on a daily basis, to the tune of many billions of dollars. We are not in the realm of ping-pong diplomacy: we are in the world of economic and cultural partnership.

These many cooperative projects require trust, credibility, and commitment—all of which were lacking between the United States and the Soviet Union. During the Cold War, the only meaningful sense in which the antagonists cooperated was in maintaining an international system designed to manage their competition, and in their implicit (though unstable) agreement not to attack each other. Even at the height of détente, cooperation was focused on reducing the likelihood of nuclear conflict and recognizing stable borders. Otherwise the sides were implacably opposed.[14]

A major reason for the relative absence of Cold War cooperation was that the United States and the Soviet Union barely traded with each other. For each side, improving the economic status of the other would have meant weakening its own relative position. The Western and Eastern blocs were divided by borders and ideology but also by economics. Neither the Americans nor the Soviets (nor anyone else) could be confident of access to markets everywhere in the world.

By contrast, the United States and China constantly cooperate to facilitate their mutually advantageous economic relationship. Working together is the only way forward for an interdependent world built on trade. A manufacturer must care about the health of its customers. A debtor needs to worry about the state of its creditors, at least so long as it hopes to continue borrowing. The more the trade, the deeper the cooperation needed. If, for example, the United States wants to sell products in China that rely on intellectual property—films, videogames, computer programs, and pharmaceuticals—it needs China's cooperation to avoid systematic theft.[15] If China wants to invest in American companies, it must have assurances that it will be treated as well as any other investor.

Competitive Cooperation

It may seem odd to depict the economic relation between the United States and China as essentially one of cooperation. After all, American and Chinese firms compete intensely for business. The two countries compete to attract investment and create new jobs. In both places, the rhetoric of politicians often suggests the metaphor of economic warfare, with each side racing to beat the other.

The basis for treating economic competition as a form of cooperation goes back to the observation that the economic growth of some countries need not necessarily reduce the wealth of others. As the philosopher David Hume put it 250 years ago, the "jealousy of trade" is thoroughly groundless. I should not be bothered if another country gets rich. "The encrease [sic] of riches and commerce in any one nation, instead of hurting, commonly promotes the riches and commerce of all its neighbors."[16] Economic competition can make everybody better off.

In this sense, countries that participate in the international network of trade do compete, but they compete against the backdrop of collective cooperation that creates mutual benefits. The definition of a freely chosen bargain is that each side is better off making the trade than not making it. What is more, some basic rules of exchange must apply for agreement even to be possible: the parties must agree on a currency, and they must trust each other to make payment. The participants in an international trade system can thus be compared to citizens within one country. They compete with each other to get rich while also jointly cooperating in governance that leaves them all better off than they would be without it.

This close, interdependent relationship makes war between the participants seem unlikely because it would be irrational. Should a creditor nation attack a debtor, it would destroy the value of its own assets. Invading your trading partners would mean the end of trade until the war was over, and beyond.

This observation was first made famous by a British journalist named Norman Angell, who in 1909 published *The Great Illusion,* an enormously popular, widely read book, arguing that the arms race between Britain and Germany was the result of a fundamental mistake.[17] Each side seemed to believe that economic success was dependent upon military dominance. But modern economic power derived from a capitalist system based on credit. In a world of debt, conquering another country was useless, because the wealth of the conquered country would evaporate at the moment of conquest.

World War I came despite Angell's insistence on its irrationality, and Angell's argument seemed to have been discredited. But it was revived in the 1970s in a more sophisticated form by liberal scholars of foreign relations, who argued that economic interdependence, international institutions, and democratization could sharply reduce the likelihood of war.[18] The liberal internationalists' most impressive evidence is the European Union, which brought peace (and most of the time, prosperity) to countries who were perennial enemies as recently as World War II and for hundreds of years before that. The European Union achieved its miracle by gradually increasing members' mutual economic ties while embedding them deeper and deeper in institutions of law and government. One reason it is so difficult to imagine war among Britain, France, and Germany today is that they all have too much collective prosperity to lose.

A crucial internationalist lesson of the post–World War II period is that great economic powers do not inevitably become great military powers. Before the war, Germany and Japan had both grown fast and become major global actors. After defeating them, the United States (with the acquiescence of the Soviet Union) imposed nonmilitarization on each. The idea was that, even if they became economic challengers, they would not be able to function as strategic challengers ever again.

It worked. Embedded within the European Union, Germany

gradually returned to a dominant regional economic position, but without the expansionist aspirations that had accompanied its rise as a nation-state. Even after German reunification, Germany has remained committed to the peaceful ideal of a European project. It focuses on wealth, not military might.

In postwar Japan, too, rapid economic growth took place without any corresponding impulse to domination. When Japan's economy was reaching its zenith in the 1980s, it sparked nationalist worries in the United States about Japanese firms buying American businesses. But no one seriously feared that Japan was about to reemerge as a contender for a new military empire of its own. Despite, or perhaps because of, Japan's recent imperial past, there has as yet been no significant movement in Japan to turn the country into an armed global power.[19]

Neither post–World War II success story would have been possible without the aegis of U.S. military protection during the Cold War.[20] It helped, too, that neither country could have begun a military buildup without having it quashed by the United States. As the Axis, they had tried the route of global dominance and been defeated. Yet within this new demilitarized framework, Germany and Japan pursued rational strategies of economic growth without geostrategic ambition. When it was no longer possible for them to be important military players, their long-term interests no longer dictated that they try to be.

Rise and Reason

Is China today like the rebuilt Germany or Japan, a rising economic power with no particular reason to seek military preeminence and risk conflict with the United States? Brazil, Russia, and India, the other fast-growing so-called BRIC countries, seem to fit this description. Brazil has no tradition of global military ambition, and its location lends it the option of continental leadership but little more. On top of this, its growth slowed considerably more than the other BRICs' in 2011 and 2012. Russia's degraded infrastructure, its rampant corruption, and not least, its status as a defeated superpower, stand in the way of Russian regeneration to anything like its prior position, despite Vladimir Putin's nationalism and its remaining nuclear weapons.

India, occupying most of a subcontinent, does have a history of fighting with its important neighbors, including, in 1962, with China. Its nuclear arsenal, pointing primarily toward Pakistan, is a marker of its great power status. Yet despite its impressive economic growth, nearly as rapid as China's, India is limited by poverty, of both people and infrastructure. Democracy lends stability and confers other important benefits, but it can actually hamper major infrastructure development. Partly as a result, India's growth has not been industrial. Driven by technology, it has not generated very many new jobs. Increasingly, India has a sophisticated global business elite sitting atop a crumbling infrastructure. This is not a recipe for becoming a superpower.

It could be argued that China's situation is also roughly analogous to that of postwar Germany and Japan. A trade-based economy depends on global stability, which could be disrupted by an attempt to become a military force. Some sophisticated analysts think that it would be strategically foolish for China to try to compete with American military dominance while simultaneously trying to grow its economy.[21]

What is more, seen from the standpoint of economic interdependence, military conflict between the United States and China would seem to be as mutually irrational as a war today among European powers. Unless and until China can develop an internal consumer market with massive buying power, no one other than the United States will have a comparably insatiable appetite for its goods. Unless it massively increases revenue or reduces social welfare entitlement, the United States will still have to borrow, which means that it will need cash-rich countries like China to loan it the money. With $136,000 of debt per household and a one-to-one ratio of debt to GDP, the United States needs to borrow cheaply to keep its economy healthy.

Close economic ties create the possibility of economic warfare. It would be extraordinarily costly for China if the United States closed its markets to Chinese products. Indeed, if China suddenly lost a quarter of its revenue, the resulting economic wallop could destabilize the rule of the Chinese Communist Party. It would also be dangerous for the United States if China began to dump its U.S. bonds. China would lose a lot of money along the way, but conceivably such a loss of confidence in the credit of the U.S. government could make it more expensive for the United States to borrow elsewhere.

Even if economic warfare were partial, rather than total, as in a limited trade war, the negative consequences would be substantial. Given the depth of their interdependence, *any* breakdown in economic relations between the United States and China could be disastrous. Trade war, the manipulation of financial markets, and escalating economic cyber attack—all would have tremendous, if unknown, destructive capacity.

The gravity and uncertainty of these dangers make them unlikely to happen. The costs would be so high that many consider such possibilities to be the stuff of fantasy, too self-destructive to occur in the real world. Just as mutually assured nuclear destruction helped keep the U.S.-Soviet conflict in check during the Cold War, runs the argument, mutually assured economic destruction—or at least something like it—should keep the United States and China away from major, direct economic warfare. If no one can win a war, and if both sides know it in advance, it would be literally mad to fight it.

For the foreseeable future, the U.S.-China economic relationship is going to remain a tight mutual embrace. That gives China a good reason to avoid trying to become a global superpower if doing so would increase the risks of conflict with the United States. In the long run, China would like to rely less on exports and to diversify its customer base, both to increase its own stability and to worry less about the cost of a potential trade war. The United States would prefer a more dispersed ownership of its debt in order to avoid the leverage that can come from a single creditor. But for now, each side is stuck.[22]

The Question of History

In the past, close economic ties between rising and dominant powers have not always managed to stave off conflict between them.[23] The great powers of Europe traded extensively with one another in the years before World War I. Their economies were deeply interlinked. Germany, which was conceived by Britons as the most significant potential challenger to their global position, was an important trading partner of the United Kingdom.[24]

Yet the extent of trade between Germany and imperial Britain was still substantially less than that of the United States and China today. Germany's economy was not dependent upon exports. The British economy, which was export-driven, had a highly diversified customer base, of which Germany was only a proportionate part.[25] Norman Angell's arguments for the irrationality of conflict depended upon a much broader, global economic interdependence, rather than upon the mutual dependence of the two crucial competitors.

In this same era, the United States, another rising power, did trade with Britain on a scale comparable to the U.S.-China trade of our time. The United States sent roughly half of its exports to Britain between 1885 and 1895. Over the next two decades the proportion declined, but it still remained at around one-quarter on the eve of World War I and held steady during the war years. Britain, for its part, exported between 10 and 15 percent of its products to the United States during the same pre–World War I period.[26]

It is a little puzzling that the British Empire did not in this era (or ever, in fact) see the United States as its most significant strategic threat, the empire that would ultimately succeed it.[27] But the United States was not disturbing the balance of power in Europe as Germany was. Its expanding spheres of influence were in the Pacific and Latin America, where Britain's imperial ambitions were relatively mild.[28] Indeed, the United States in the modern era never fought a war against the United Kingdom. It took Britain's part in both world wars and inherited the position of global superpower only after the British Empire suffered such great damage as a result of those wars.

There was also no deep ideological divide between the United States and the United Kingdom, two liberal democracies committed to capitalism and free trade. If anything, British imperialists saw the potential American empire as a kind of adjunct to their own, sparing them the expense of expanding still further. When in 1898 the United States took the Philippines, Guam, and Puerto Rico in the Spanish-American War, Britain alone among the European powers supported it. Rudyard Kipling responded the next year with his famous poem, "The White Man's Burden," which (unless read ironically) applauded America's newfound Pacific imperialism.[29]

Economically, the current relationship between the United States and China is even deeper than was that between the United States and the United Kingdom. Governments of earlier eras did not typically own the debts of other sovereign nations. The central banks of the United States and Britain rarely held each other's treasury bonds. The idea of a sovereign wealth fund that would seek simultaneously to make money in capital markets and advance its owners' national interests was still far in the future.[30]

Foreign bondholders have long influenced governments, pushing for fiscal and constitutional reforms. One could write a history of constitutional change in the light of market pressures and incentives. But foreign nationals' ownership of a country's debt is different from a foreign government's ownership of a high percentage of outstanding government bonds. The interdependence between nations runs much deeper when the bondholder is not a private banker but a government that cannot afford for the debtor to default. And the influence that the bondholder might exercise over the creditor nation is correspondingly much greater.

In essence, then, the argument that the United States and China will not find themselves in a military conflict for global power depends on one basic, historical fact: never before has the dominant world power been so economically interdependent with the rising challenger it must confront. Under these conditions, trade and debt provide overwhelming economic incentives to avoid conflict that would be costly to all. Over time the mutual interests of the two countries will outweigh any tensions that arise between them. Anything else would simply be irrational.

If only the world were so simple.

CHAPTER TWO

DOOMED TO CONFLICT

Tsai Ing-wen does not look like the sort of person who would cause World War III. A youthful fifty-seven-year-old with glasses and a sensible bob, she appears to be just what she is—the very model of a reasonable, successful Taiwanese politician. A former law professor, she holds advanced degrees from Cornell and the London School of Economics. In 2012, she was the unsuccessful presidential candidate of the Democratic Progressive Party, winning more than 47 percent of the votes cast.

But had Tsai's DPP won, tensions across the Taiwan Strait could have become very high very fast. Like some 55 percent of Taiwanese (the figure is higher among younger people), Tsai favors the formal independence of Taiwan from China.[1] To the Chinese Communist Party, the very idea of Taiwanese independence is a casus belli. China's best offer is one state, two systems. Fully two-thirds of Taiwanese citizens consider this option "unacceptable."[2]

Over time, Taiwanese voters may come to terms with the reality of their situation and soften their attitude toward becoming part of China. But it is more likely that most Taiwanese will do no such thing. Taiwan is a democracy whose citizens enjoy robust free speech and free political choice. Its economy is healthy, and it is able to benefit from its proximity to China through an extensive trade regime that is the very epitome of cool war contradiction.[3] Why wouldn't ordinary Taiwanese want to maintain their freedoms alongside their economic well-being?

Of all the potential flashpoints for real violent conflict between the United States and China, Taiwan is the scariest. A future Taiwanese politician might well get elected on a platform of active independence. At the same time, Chinese leaders might wish to shore up their legitimacy by distracting their public from a lagging economy. A hawkish leader with close ties to the People's Liberation Army could send a new Chinese aircraft carrier into the strait. The president of the United States would then face an immediate and pressing dilemma: to respond in kind, inviting war, or to hold back and compromise sole global superpower status in an instant.

The Cuban missile crisis looked a lot like this. At the tensest moment of the Cold War, 1960s-era secrecy gave John Kennedy and his advisers several days to pick a course of action. Today the decision would have to come in hours—or even minutes.

Realism and the Case for Conflict

Given that the United States and China are so economically interdependent, why do many veteran observers of international affairs believe they are doomed to inevitable conflict? The answer does not lie merely in the closing wealth gap between the countries. Although the size of its economy is fast approaching that of the United States, China is not yet rich by American and European standards, and it has much ground to cover before its GDP measured per capita is anywhere near that of the United States. Its economic growth is not in itself a threat but a reason for celebration, an opportunity to alleviate some of the world's deepest poverty.

The basis for the conviction that conflict is coming lies in the all-important difference between China and the other existing and emerging global economic powers. None of today's other fast-growing states has the capacity to become a global power able to compete militarily with the United States. The economic rise of India or Brazil might change the balance of trade worldwide, but it will not change the balance of power.

In stark contrast, China's combination of growth, geographical position, size, and history means that if it chooses to, it can make a bid to become a global superpower. The fact that China could realistically try to change the global distribution of power opens the door to a further possibility: that it is in China's interests to change the way strategic power is now allocated globally.

It is never in anyone's interest to try to do the impossible. Rebuilt Germany and Japan after World War II might have wished to become global superpowers, but the United States and the Soviet Union would have stopped them, so it was not in their interests even to think about trying. China, however, has the option of pursuing superpower status. That requires us to ask what China *should* do in order to find out what China *will* do.

On the surface, it may seem perverse to ask whether China ought to become a global superpower. Shouldn't we be asking instead whether China wants to become a global superpower? Isn't the decision ultimately up to its leaders and citizens?

The reason to begin with China's capacities and interests, rather than its subjective desires, has to do with an influential, realist vision of how countries act in the international sphere. In his recent book *On China*, Henry Kissinger, the single most influential American observer of China for forty years—and an inveterate realist—explains the problem by reference to a 1907 memorandum written by the British bureaucrat Eyre Crowe. Crowe's secret memorandum claimed that Germany would try to end Britain's world dominance as the necessary result of its economic growth and its disruption of the existing balance of power. It did not matter what

Germany's political class subjectively wanted, or that much global wealth would be destroyed by the use of force: war was coming as the result of conflicting interests.[4] And of course, Crowe was right, not only about World War I but also about World War II.

Today's foreign policy realists have added more nuance to the notion of national interest that arguably goes back to Thucydides's famous assertion that the Peloponnesian War was caused by Sparta's worry about the rise of Athens.[5] Interests must be understood in terms of the multiple, sometimes conflicting goals of various domestic political and economic actors. Germans of the aristocratic warrior class, for example, might have sought war, while others, whose business interests depended on international ties, might have opposed it.[6]

Many realists are also open to considering the role of ideology in shaping how countries act. The most enlightened have noticed that because interests are a species of ideas, it matters not simply what they are but what we rightly or wrongly believe them to be. And all realists have in common an abiding belief that those who can get power for themselves almost invariably try to do so.[7] If China can significantly improve its power position in the world and would benefit by doing so, it will.

From a realist perspective, China's economic rise, accompanied by America's relative economic decline, does change the balance of power. It changes that balance fundamentally, because it gives China the means, opportunity, and motive to alter the global arrangement in which the United States is the world's sole superpower. According to the logic of realism, the two countries are therefore already at odds in a struggle for geopolitical dominance. One is the established superpower, the other its leading challenger. Under the circumstances, a shooting war is not unavoidable—but conflict is.

The Taiwan Option

How could China, if it so chose, become a global superpower capable of challenging the United States? It is undisputed that the People's Liberation Army is nowhere close to matching the U.S. military. But this fact is deceptive. To alter the balance of power in a fundamental way, China does not need to reach military parity with the United States.

To see how superpower status can emerge without parity, all that is needed is to focus on Taiwan, which represents China's overwhelming military priority.[8] A rich and important country with close historical links to China, Taiwan is also a close U.S. military ally. Acquiring Taiwan would be extremely valuable to China, both geostrategically and economically. China's desire to incorporate Taiwan into its political orbit is probably the most significant symbolic or ideological component of its foreign policy. So far China has been able to dissuade Taiwan from declaring independence. But as things stand between the two countries, Taiwan cannot be reunited into China without at least the implicit threat of force.[9]

Until the United States formally established diplomatic relations with China, the protection of Taiwan was one of America's leading treaty commitments. Since President Jimmy Carter unilaterally annulled the Taiwan treaty in 1979, U.S. policy on the protection of Taiwan has taken the form of "strategic ambiguity." No formal commitment binds the United States to intervene on Taiwan's behalf, and the exact conditions that would motivate that intervention are left intentionally unspecified. Nevertheless, Congress has passed a law requiring the president to keep it apprised of any threats to Taiwan's security. The posture of the U.S. Navy remains oriented toward protecting Taiwan from Chinese attack.

This protection is a key element of broader regional security arrangements. The alliances of the other Asian countries with the United States depend in large part on their desire not to be dominated by China. These nations would perceive U.S. abandonment of Taiwan as a signal of America's potential future abandonment of their defense. The United States therefore would give up on Taiwan only if it judged that the fight would be too costly.

From China's standpoint, the optimal strategy toward Taiwan is not a sudden confrontation in the Taiwan Strait that would agitate the U.S. public and drum up support for the defense of Taiwan. It is, rather, to build up its military capacity and acquire Taiwan without a fight. The precedent for such a process of acquisition by inevitability is China's incorporation of Hong Kong into its sovereign territory.

Hong Kong was one of the last outposts of the British Empire, and Prime Minister Margaret Thatcher intended to maintain some sort of British administration even after her country's ninety-nine-year "lease" on Hong Kong expired in 1997. In principle, Thatcher was willing to make a stand; in 1982 she had gone to war to defend the Falkland Islands, an almost entirely valueless archipelago half a world away. (Indeed, the risk to Hong Kong may have been part of Thatcher's decision to defend the Falklands against Argentina—she did not want the Chinese to believe that they could take Hong Kong with impunity.)

In the event, however, China's military capacity meant the British could not seriously contemplate fighting China the way Britain had fought (and defeated) Argentina. When Deng Xiaoping made it clear that the Chinese expected Hong Kong to revert to them, Thatcher had little choice but to agree. China offered a fig leaf in the form of "one country, two systems," allowing Britain to salvage a modicum of dignity when capitulating to the realities of power politics. But the structure was still coercive. After the meeting where Deng made China's expectation explicit, Thatcher fell down the stairs outside the Great Hall of the People.[10]

In the case of Taiwan, the idea is that the United States might be prepared to tolerate the abandonment of its historic ally—today an independent, democratic state—provided it could claim that human rights and some sort of self-government were being respected. China's goal would be to accomplish the whole process with the appearance of respecting the forms of democracy. After the United States signaled its inability or unwillingness to defend Taiwan, the people of Taiwan would, presumably, publicly acquiesce in their own absorption into China's sovereign sphere. After all, like the United States, they would have no choice.

To see why this scenario is so plausible, all that is required is to ask the following question: Would the president of the United States go to war with China over Taiwan absent some high-profile, immediate crisis capable of mobilizing domestic support? The cost of war would be huge. No president would even contemplate such a war absent a high probability of winning it. From China's perspective, the goal would be to create a situation where the United States would not consider war as a serious option. Then China could avoid force or confrontation altogether as a direct consequence of its growing military strength.

If the United States were to abandon Taiwan, it would have to insist—to China, to Japan and South Korea, and to its own citizens—that Taiwan was in a basic sense different from the rest of Asia. To do so, it would have to accept China's longtime claim that Taiwan historically forms a part of China, despite its different language and distinctive culture. It would have to emphasize the mainland origins of Taiwan's Hokkien dialect and the presence of mainlanders on the island since 1949—indeed, all of China's rhetorical arguments for ownership. The goal would be to convince the world that the United States would fight to protect its other democratic Asian allies, just not Taiwan.

Failure to do so credibly would transform capitulation on Taiwan into the end of American military hegemony in Asia.[11] It would represent a reversal of the victories in the Pacific in World War II. It would put much of the world's economic power within

China's sphere of control, not only its sphere of influence. In short it would mean that China was on a par with the United States as a global superpower.

The Benefits of Gradual Buildup

America's credible promise to defend other Asian nations is a lot to rest upon an abstract, quasi-historical argument about whether Taiwan is "naturally" part of China. After all, Korea's ties to China were close enough that, in the sixteenth century, Korea totally Confucianized its high culture in imitation of the imperial power whose tributary it was. Japanese culture has ancient contacts with the Chinese mainland. If Taiwan is naturally part of China, then Korea and Japan are presumably part of China's "natural" sphere of influence and even control.

Thus, from the standpoint of real-world politics, the true question is how the United States can credibly commit itself to defending Japan and Korea if it chooses not to protect Taiwan. Through the implacable logic of realpolitik, the problem is immediate rather than potential. The moment it becomes possible to imagine the United States giving up Taiwan, it is already necessary for the United States to offer some believable signal that it would protect its other allies.

That moment of imagination has already arrived: although U.S. defense experts might think otherwise, many close watchers of U.S. domestic policy can conceive of a compromise on Taiwan that would restore Chinese sovereignty. The future is now. For the United States to concede Asia to China's domination would entail stepping down from being the world's sole superpower to being one of two competing superpowers. But notice what this means. The only way the United States can credibly commit itself to the protection of its Asian allies is for the United States to remain committed to sole-superpower status. That sounds easy—so long as it does not involve any costs. The reality is hard. To be the sole super-power, you must be prepared to fight to keep that position.

China, for its part, need only grow its military capacity to the point where it would be big enough not to have to use it. When two rational opponents face each other, the relative size of their militaries can tell them most of what they need to know about who would win any war and at what cost. They can then adjust the relations of power between them based on the new military realities—all without going to war. Observers of Chinese military strategy sometimes refer to the Chinese strategic preference for "encirclement" rather than direct confrontation, as though this were some uniquely Chinese viewpoint.[12] Actually, the best way to win a war is always by making your opponent capitulate before anyone has fired a shot. Encirclement is simply the Chinese version of this approach.

All this does not mean that China will or should enter into an immediate war footing with the United States. Military rise takes place over decades, not months. Too fast a buildup would spook the United States and encourage hawkish anti-Chinese sentiment there. Complete secrecy with regard to such a major buildup would be impossible. Theorists of international relations would say that, even if the buildup were hidden, its existence could be logically deduced from the fact of China's interests. But China nevertheless has reason to convince the American public that its intentions are not hostile. China also enjoys the advantage that the United States, as a democracy, may not pay sufficient attention to the military maneuvers of its potential challenger.

Much better to advance as quietly as possible for as long as possible, then emerge with increased military might as a fait accompli. The party has done a good job of convincing the Chinese public that the nation's rise must proceed slowly, with economic growth first. It helps that the party is not subjected to the electoral cycles of democratic governments, with the limited time horizon that such a structure imposes.

The other reason to build up slowly is more basic. In terms of technology and capacity, China's military remains some distance behind the United States—though probably not decades behind, as claimed by Chinese experts eager to damp down U.S. fears. Building a large, effective, and technologically sophisticated military is a time-consuming and extremely expensive business. One of China's relative advantages over the United States in terms of economic growth is that it appears not to expend a comparable percentage of its GDP on defense. It must avoid the Soviet mistake of overspending to keep up in an arms race. Better to get rich and then spend as you grow than to spend and run the risk of not getting rich enough. The risk of overexpenditure on defense is especially great in a system where many economic resources still belong to the state and private industry lacks the political clout to resist government spending. The optimal approach for China is to increase its military capacity at roughly the same rate as its economic growth, thereby keeping its increased military strength sustainable.

As the Taiwan scenario shows, China does not need to achieve military parity with the U.S. military to join the United States as a global superpower. All it needs is to be powerful enough to deter the United States from fighting it over Taiwan. Most surprising of all, it may be there already.

Diverging Interests

So China could realistically become a global superpower capable of standing up to the United States in Asia. But does the United States have any interest in trying to stop this from happening? And beyond the benefits of acquiring Taiwan, is it in China's interests to aim for this end?

The United States has a fundamental interest in retaining the status of sole global superpower that it inherited after the collapse of the Soviet Union. The benefits of being alone at number one are both psychic and practical. Power may not be the most elemental human impulse, but it is among the most important. A nation whose power is on a different scale from all others can protect its citizens more effectively (and more recklessly) than any other. Almost by definition, a nation with that much power can make states and peoples do things that they otherwise would not want to do. It can, if it chooses, dictate much of the distribution of power in every region on earth, threatening those whom it does not persuade to become its friends.

To Americans, knowledge of their dominance affords some degree of comfort in an uncertain and changing world. Politicians in a nationalist democracy do not get elected by telling the voters that they may not always belong to the greatest nation on earth. Whatever it may fear in its heart of hearts, the U.S. public insists that the country must sustain its leading position, not lose it. Perhaps, like Britons, Americans might someday have to learn what it means to be a former superpower. But that eventuality is still far off, and it will not happen without a fight.

In concrete terms, being the sole global superpower confers material benefits. To take one salient example, today the U.S. dollar is the global reserve currency. Not by coincidence, there has been one other global reserve currency in the modern era: the British pound sterling, during the period of British global dominance. Although the magnitude of the effect is uncertain, the United States is able to borrow more cheaply than it otherwise would because other countries need dollars to hold in reserve.[13]

A related material benefit of superpower status is the global demand for U.S. Treasury bonds, which investors consider the safest harbor when global economic confidence is shaken. Remarkably, the so-called flight to quality seems to happen even when the source of nervousness is the credit of the U.S. government itself. When in the summer of 2011, newly elected Tea Party congressmen brought the country to the edge of default, interest rates on Treasury bills actually went down rather than up. The fact that people around the world continue to buy U.S. debt at historically low rates is an indicator of how useful it is to be the sole superpower. The purchasers believe that the United States is too big to fail, a belief that derives from the role that the United States plays in the world order. For the United States to lose the benefit of the free financial ride that comes from geopolitical power would be significant.

Meanwhile, China's long-term geopolitical interest lies in removing the United States from the position of sole global superpower. Again, the reasons are both psychological and material. Like the United States, China is a continental power with vast reach. It has a glorious imperial history, including regional dominance of what was, for China, much of the known world. In the same way that the United States is proud of democracy and its global spread, China has its own rich civilizational ideal, Confucianism. During the years of China's ascendance, the cultures of Taiwan, Japan, Korea, and Vietnam—sometimes called the Sinosphere—were deeply influenced by Chinese ideas. Confucianism still plays a meaningful part in the thinking of at least 1.7 billion people.[14]

The Chinese public is deeply nationalist, which matters to China's unelected political leadership as much as U.S. nationalism does to American politicians. The people of China feel a deep pride in their rapid economic rise and their enhanced global position. As China becomes the world's largest economy, there is meaningful public pressure for its power status to advance in parallel. Any alternative would be humiliating. And as all Chinese know, China has suffered its share of humiliation in the last two centuries.

China also has concrete strategic interests that are blocked by U.S. dominance. Chief among them is its desire to bring Taiwan into its national orbit, a core interest that would be easily achievable if Taiwan were not protected by the United States. More broadly, it is in China's interest—and eventual capacity—to return to its onetime historical place as the dominant regional power in Asia, where the United States has held sway since World War II.[15]

This does not mean making Japan or South Korea into part of China. It does mean eventually replacing the existing regional security system that is designed to contain and balance it. Right now, China lacks the military capacity to bring this about, and so it would be against China's interests to speak openly about its goals. But the increasingly belligerent conflicts over small islands in the East and South China Seas are products of the fact that everybody knows it. Barack Obama's autumn 2011 trip to Asia, when he committed the United States to focusing its military presence in the region, was meant as a first response acknowledging the reality of China's interest.

In economic terms, China believes that it pays a price for the dollar functioning as the global reserve currency. The global position of the dollar gives the Federal Reserve the ability to print money (through the policy of quantitative easing), thus diluting Chinese dollar holdings without China having a strong alternative place to park its money or a way to purchase commodities. China openly states its long-term goal of diversifying the global reserve so that other currencies or newly created international financial instruments could fill some of the function that the dollar now does.

What remains unsaid is that weakening the dollar as a global reserve currency would be very difficult to do without weakening American geopolitical power. The markets must trust any new reserve currencies. That means they must believe that the issuers are overwhelmingly likely to survive any sort of international crisis. If the geopolitical security of those issuers is, however, guaranteed by the United States, then in effect they are in American hands. To imagine a global reserve currency in another form is to imagine that the geopolitical power of the United States has been balanced by other actors.

The Evidence

In realist terms, China's interest in becoming a global superpower, and its capacity to do so, suggest that it will seek to become a global superpower. Lee Kuan Yew, the Singaporean leader who has been a mentor to every major Chinese leader since Deng Xiaoping, was recently asked if China's leaders intend to displace the United States as Asia's preeminent power. "Of course," Lee replied. "Why not? . . . Their reawakened sense of destiny is an overpowering force." Indeed, Lee explained bluntly, "It is China's intention to become the greatest power in the world."[16]

There is plenty of hard evidence to support this interpretation. China's defense budget has grown by more than 10 percent for several years, rising officially to $116 billion in the most recent published reports, with actual defense spending as high as $180 billion.[17] In 2011 China bought its first aircraft carrier (a refitted Soviet model), announced plans to build several more, and openly tested its first stealth aircraft. In 2012, party-controlled media acknowledged more ambitious plans to develop ballistic missiles that would carry multiple warheads—and therefore be able to get around the U.S. missile defense shield. China is also working on submarine-fired missiles that would avoid U.S. early-warning systems left over from the Cold War.[18] It is building up its space program on both the civilian and military sides.[19]

In its public rhetoric, China speaks longingly of a more multipolar world less dominated by the United States. Influential voices in China's military establishment and among its defense intellectuals argue openly that China should aim to become the world's greatest power.[20] In practice, China acts like a state intent on bringing its geostrategic position in line with its economic one.

Conventional military growth is only one facet of China's effort to change its power relationship to the United States. Cyber war, a fast-developing new front in global conflict, is another. In the fall of 2012, the U.S. secretary of defense warned of a "cyber Pearl Harbor" that would paralyze U.S. infrastructure targets, which he said foreign actors had been actively trying to penetrate with some success.[21] Experts believe that the Chinese government launches thousands of cyber attacks a year against U.S. targets as important as the natural gas pipelines. As the secretary hinted, the United States is developing not merely defensive but offensive cyber warfare tools in return.[22] Reports suggest that the U.S. military's cyber command will quintuple in size to some five thousand members in the near future—and that does not count the intelligence operators who are already in the business.

Cyber attacks are an especially fruitful method from the Chinese perspective. Because they do not (yet) involve traditional military mobilization, they exploit a dimension in which U.S. and Chinese power are more symmetrical. They involve a certain amount of deniability, as efforts can be made to mask the origin of attacks, making attribution difficult. They may have a significant economic upside, especially if they involve theft of intellectual property from American firms. Cyber war takes place largely in secret, unknown to the general public on both sides. Best of all for China, the rules for cyber war are still very much in flux. That means public retaliation is still extremely unlikely, reducing the danger of public embarrassment if things go badly. Regular cyber attacks are therefore likely to be an ongoing facet of a cool war.[23]

For China, then, chipping away at U.S. power and closing the gap is a long-term project, not one that can be accomplished overnight. Nevertheless, it has identifiable, measurable objectives along the way. China must gradually increase its military position in the East and South China Seas. At present, the United States dominates the region through its security arrangements with Taiwan, Japan, and South Korea. For China to displace the United States in this arrangement, it must avoid antagonizing its neighbors to the point where they cling closer to the United States. China has to convince the other countries that very close economic relations among them make it the best guarantor of regional security. Above all, it must convince countries accustomed to operating under U.S. protection that in the long run, the United States may not be able to protect them.

Nationalism and the National Interest

The Diaoyu (or in Japanese, Senkaku) Islands are five forlorn, un-inhabited piles of rock in the East China Sea, located some 120 miles from Taiwan and some 200 from the closest bits of China and Japan. Controlled by Japan, they are also claimed by China and Taiwan. Beginning in the summer of 2012, they became the site of a surreal international drama.

First a series of fishing vessels landed civilians, who variously raised the flags of China, Taiwan, and eventually Japan. The particular Japanese flag chosen was especially surprising: it was the old rising sun of the Japanese Empire before World War II. In the wake of these events, the regional government of Tokyo moved to purchase the islands from the family that Japan recognizes as its private owners—over furious Chinese objections. In response, China sent out patrol boats manned by China Marine Surveillance, a kind of parallel coast guard, with the express purpose of asserting sovereignty.

The escalation that followed was quick and quickly military. China sent a pair of its own, Chinese-made J-10 fighter jets; Japan replied with American-made F-15s. The U.S. Senate adopted a resolution pledging to help Japan defend the islands against armed attack. The ordinarily sober *Economist* magazine warned that China and Japan were on a course to war.[24]

The islands are strategically important because they are part of a chain running from Japan to Taiwan to Vietnam—a line roughly parallel to China's eastern coast and therefore part of China's national defense plans.[25] But the islands are not militarized, and no change in their geostrategic status had taken place. There may be oil nearby, but neither was that why citizens of three countries were so exercised. The explanation for the sentiment is something different. The islands are at the heart of a symbolic international conflict driven by nationalism.

The nationalism reflected in the controversy over the Diaoyu/Senkaku Islands is not merely some vestigial attachment to old rivalries. It is, rather, the product of geopolitical dynamics: the rise of China and the threat it now poses to neighbors who have long been protected by the United States. Whatever its status may be in Europe, nationalism is alive and well in China in particular and in Asia more broadly. It is also present in the United States, especially in relation to China. However irrational it may be on the surface, nationalism is an important and growing part of why China and the United States are finding themselves in a cool war.

For nearly two hundred years, nationalism has been the single most durable, effective legitimating force for governments and movements around the world. Nationalism is born out of confrontation. The nation must always define itself in contrast to other groupings that do not share its ethnicity, language, or state.

Having abandoned Maoist ideology, the Communist Party is on the lookout for other ways to justify its governing role. In recent years, the rapid pace of economic development has provided the legitimacy that the party needs. But the party knows perfectly well that economic development cannot be sustained at present rates forever. It needs other sources of ideological legitimacy.

The Chinese nation—whether defined in the sense of Han Chinese ethnicity or in a broader sense of multiple ethnicities living within modern China—is by a great margin the biggest nation in the history of the world. If the party can present itself to ordinary Chinese as serving the interests of the Chinese nation, it has a raison d'être even beyond merely improving citizens' individual economic well-being.

One lesson of the Cold War is that the struggle to achieve and maintain a status of global domination can sustain the attention of a nation for decades. A moment comes in the life of a nationalist ideology where, even beyond national pride, powerful feelings of connection to the national project merge with actual, real-world self-interest in achieving the goals of the nation-state. The greater the conflict, the greater will be the advantages achieved by victory. Being an American during the period of U.S. hegemony has meant reaping the fruits of citizenship in a global empire. Jobs, trade, the concentration of financial and other services, belonging to a dominant world culture—these are measurable benefits that the British enjoyed in the nineteenth century and that Americans have enjoyed in the late twentieth and early twenty-first.

For Chinese citizens experiencing a national rise, proud sentiments are only part of the story. An empowered China can actually give its citizens advantages. Being thwarted in achieving its global ambitions would mean losing prestige and benefits for Chinese people everywhere.

There is thus reason to believe that China's building nationalism would not be thwarted by an economic slowdown. It might even grow faster. Consider the example of the United States. During the Clinton years, when the economy was strong, nationalism faded as an important political force in American public life. A policy of free trade was preferred to a policy of protectionism. With the Soviet Union gone, there was no more security bogeyman on whom to focus.

The September 11 attacks generated a security-oriented nationalism that supported the wars in Afghanistan and Iraq. But even this nationalism had a missionizing quality, since it was coupled with the aspiration to spread democracy in the Middle East. Official U.S. rhetoric treated the Afghan and Iraqi peoples as potential allies, unfortunately subjected to the tyrannies of the Taliban and Saddam Hussein. Anti-Muslim sentiment certainly existed in the United States, but it was not focally directed at any one nation-state.

The global recession and the simultaneous rise of China have changed this situation. China has become a target, blamed for artificially depressing its currency and increasing the U.S. trade deficit. Impetus to protect U.S. industry from defeat at the hands of outside competition is growing. Barack Obama's bailout of the U.S. automakers belonged to the realm of economic policy, but it was economic policy powerfully informed by a sense of national pride.

As the United States continues to struggle economically, we can expect increasing nationalism from its citizens and the politicians who represent them. Nationalism, after all, deflects attention away from the internal causes of problems and toward external sources of trouble. It rallies citizens in the common cause of advancing their collective interests. It can provide a source of hope to people whose economic future is uncertain.

These conditions strongly suggest that the competitive, psychological dimensions of U.S.-China conflict will grow in future years. Beyond the divergent interests of the two countries, leaders in each will find reasons to blame the other. The dynamic of eager rise and reluctant fall creates perfect conditions for making conflict a reality. Economic interdependence will mitigate this conflict—but cannot eliminate it altogether.

CHAPTER THREE

A ONE-SIDED WAR OF IDEAS

The Cold War was a battle of ideals. Communism and liberal democracy each claimed the moral high ground, and each claimed to be superior in practice. As systems, they were mutually exclusive. Only one side could win.

Will the cool war be ideological in the same way? Today, is either China or the United States advocating a universal ideology meant to apply to everyone everywhere? If not, then perhaps in the absence of ideological struggle, the two nations could craft a kind of competitive partnership. Each would have its sphere of influence and shared responsibility for maintaining global security and stability. An Asia dominated by China could be counterbalanced by a West dominated by the United States. Everyone would get along. There would be neither cold war nor cool war. Each would be a "responsible stakeholder" in the international system, as Robert Zoellick, George W. Bush's deputy secretary of state, optimistically put it in 2007.

This scenario of shared maintenance of the international order sounds appealing. For the United States, after all, being the sole superpower has had its drawbacks. The financial burden of maintaining global stability has been high. Even more costly have been America's unforced errors during two decades of unquestioned dominance. A strategic counterpart might help keep it honest. One reason that the United States invaded Iraq and Afghanistan was that it could.

But if cool war ideologies are sufficiently universal and mutually exclusive, they will pose genuine barriers to peaceful, cooperative strategic coexistence. Ideas about how people should be governed and what states are for exert a tremendous influence on international politics. Political ideas are among the tools we use to define what our interests are. These ideas can be even more important than what realists describe as enduring interests. In international affairs, as in every area of life, interests are not facts like the laws of nature. They are, rather, objectives that we choose based on our ideas—the product of what we believe our interests to be.

Of course, countries with very different political ideas and systems cooperate with one another for mutual benefit. The United States and Saudi Arabia have been close allies for decades despite the fact that one is a democracy with no established religion and the other is an Islamic monarchy. Each side has something the other wants. The United States offers security and a market, and Saudi Arabia offers oil. Even countries at war with each other can reach limited agreements in narrow domains.[1]

But when political ideologies are opposed and aggressive, then any accommodation cannot be more than temporary—an opportunity for both sides to gather resources for the final battle between them. Cooperation strengthens the enemy and is therefore not to be undertaken except under limited, exceptional circumstances and to avoid disastrous breakdown, like the modest cooperation between the Soviet Union and the United States during the Cold War.

Peace and the Problem of Ideology

From the standpoint of China, there is today much less ideological difference between itself and the West than there was during the Cold War. The Chinese Communist Party is still Chinese and is definitely a ruling party, but it is no longer ideologically communist in any of the traditional senses of the term. Judged by its behavior and rhetoric, the party no longer believes in an essentially Marxist picture of economic relations. Mao's economic ideas have been reinterpreted out of existence.

What remains—the core ideology of the Chinese Communist Party today—is an experimental pragmatism in economics and politics alike, best captured by the much-publicized aphorism of transformative leader Deng Xiaoping: "It doesn't matter if the cat is white or black; if it catches mice, it's a good cat."[2] The leadership of the party is prepared to try anything that may enhance development and Chinese national strength. Even the goal of maintaining the position of the party, which is obviously in the self-interest of its members, is understood in pragmatic, practical terms.

Having known in the recent past what it is to be a deeply ideological power, China's political elites have come honestly to their view that political ideology does not much matter. China's new generation of leaders lived through the Cultural Revolution. This was their formative experience of political oppression, whether they played the role of empowered Red Guards or of young people sent down to rural villages to perform years of manual labor. Most of the current leadership had both experiences in succession and did not get to attend college until they were in their twenties. They recognize that political circumstances can change quickly and that the consequences of power shifts can be bloody. They believe that pragmatism, whatever its drawbacks, has marked an enormous improvement in China over ideological commitment.

This pragmatism is captured in the party's attitude toward democracy, rights, and the rule of law. All were, at one time, condemned by orthodox communism as adjuncts to capitalism. Today it is difficult to find implacable opposition in Chinese official circles to any of these admittedly flexible ideals. Now that capitalism is no longer the definitive enemy of communism, the elements of democratic rule need not be seen as technologies for legitimating an unjust, exploitative system. As a result, the Chinese government is willing to experiment with elements of government systems that will continue to enhance development without radically threatening the stability of an already unstable system. Some officials have published books with titles like *Democracy Is a Good Thing*.[3]

In retrospect, the crackdown on the democracy protesters at Tiananmen Square did not mark a principled rejection of the ideals of democracy. It rejected the practical implementation of democracy in real time. The senior party leadership was deciding that immediate democratization would lead to collapse. A glance at the Soviet Union suggests that, however immoral their judgment may have been, it was also probably correct. Democratization was the handmaiden of Soviet dissolution. In the case of Russia, rapid democratization also turned out to be highly impermanent.[4]

China's ideological pragmatism means that it is prepared to engage in political cooperation with democracies, so long as those democracies are willing to respect China's way of doing things. Chinese nationalism is still a potential barrier to close political cooperation. But as the European Union has demonstrated, it can be possible to negotiate close, long-term strategic relationships—and to share some governance—even when people are nationalists. The bottom line is that, seen from China's perspective, the ideological divide of the present is much less significant than that of the Cold War.

From the perspective of the West, however, the ideological divide in today's cool war resembles that of the Cold War. Democracy, human rights, and the rule of law are not simply pragmatic mechanisms for allowing people to live well. To the contrary, for most Westerners these are crucial components of a morally obligatory governing system.

Seen from this angle, the fact that China is, practically speaking, no longer communist is nice but not enough. China is not democratic and does not appear to be on the road to democracy. Many in the West believe that policy toward China should be structured around the goal of making democracy, human rights, and the rule of law into China's governing norms. Indeed, it is no exaggeration to say that many Westerners, including Western political leaders, believe that China's present governing system is fundamentally illegitimate. They reject the right of the party to govern and would prefer to see China's political regime replaced with something altogether different.

These beliefs pose a challenge to the possibility of peaceful strategic coexistence between two superpowers. Think of it from the Chinese leaders' point of view: they must engage with opposite numbers who would like to see their whole governing structure crumble.[5] Their Western negotiating partners think they hold their place at the table unjustly. Given this reality, they must accept that any deal made by their Western interlocutors is meant as a step, however small, toward their own destruction. This is not a good starting point for mutual trust or respect.

Ideological conflict on one side might be better than the mutual ideological revulsion of the Cold War. But it is still profoundly destabilizing. And its source is not China. It is the West.

Western Values

How flexible is the Western commitment to the universality of law, democracy, and human rights? The possibility that the cool war might be an ideological conflict because of Western beliefs calls for considering those beliefs more carefully. The goal should be to make and keep the peace if at all possible, not to assume that conflict is predetermined. Can the core Western beliefs in question be understood in ways that would reduce conflict with China rather than generate it?

Breaking down the system of liberal democracy into its component parts can help provide the answer. While some compromise is possible, the Western ideological commitment to these ideas is so powerful that the United States could not ultimately tolerate the emergence of credible alternatives on a global scale. To the extent that the United States perceives China as ultimately unwilling to move in its direction with respect to these fundamental Western values, there will be basic ideological conflict between the two sides.

The Western commitment to law is millennia older than its belief in democracy and human rights. Indeed, law may be the single value that most unifies Western historical thought. Nothing else comparably connects the ancient peoples of the Near East with those of Greece, Rome, and northern Europe. The value of law predates Christianity and arguably transcends it. When Western ideas have spread throughout the globe, whether by conquest or peaceful transition, law has always been at the forefront. In this sense, law is more than a tool for arranging human affairs. It represents the basic intellectual filter through which Westerners see the world.

Yet Western religious and philosophical tradition has always been ambivalent about law. On one hand, law seems to be the best institution for managing human society. On the other hand, applied too rigorously, it can produce absurd results. Law can fail in a crisis, and it can contradict important values like mercy, love, and even justice. The result in the real world is always a kind of unsteady compromise: the rule of law tempered with something else.[6]

Thus, when the West promotes the rule of law throughout the

world, it generally speaks as though it is promoting something it considers very useful, rather than something it believes to be inherently, universally necessary. If Westerners encountered a utopia where people got along and grew their economy without law, they might be surprised, but they would not be morally offended. In fact, such an Edenic scene has always been a Western fantasy.

As a matter of logic, therefore, the West could potentially compromise on the existence of the rule of law in other places. So long as it could preserve the rule of law for itself, it has no absolute need to export it. Western investors do have an interest in seeing their investments in China respected. But if they were confident that this would happen absent the rule of law, they would still invest to some degree. That, after all, is the situation at present from the perception of Westerners who do business in China today.

What Westerners almost surely could not tolerate, however, would be the global spread of a nonlegal or antilegal conception of governance and property. It is one thing to observe wonderingly that China has grown despite the absence of stable, legal property rights of the kind that Westerners expect to see in successful countries. It would be quite another if copycat countries began to claim that the Chinese way would work for them as well. This would ignite fear in the West that the rule of law might be eroded domestically. Fear of this possibility is a reason that the United States can be expected to continue advocating ideologically for the rule of law in China.

On the Chinese side, there is also an ambivalent attitude toward law. Some activists within the Chinese elite believe firmly that the rule of law is necessary to stabilize property rights, combat corruption, and continue economic growth. Not surprisingly, these same activists are often the ones who are most (carefully) critical of Communist Party rule and eagerly anticipate the transformation of China into a multiparty democracy.[7]

Within the party itself, many thinkers realize that there is a difference between the rule *of* law, which implies that the law is above the party, and rule *by* law, which suggests that the party could use law as a technology to improve governance under its authority. Some voices within the party are strongly in favor of expanding the use of law to regularize institutions. In a 2012 white paper sketching its policy on law, the party quasi-officially called for greater respect for judicial decisions. In the coded language of Chinese reform, this seems to have signaled recognition of the need for more rule-based legal practice.[8]

This pro-law view, however, is not at all universally acknowledged within the party. The basic structure of legal decision making in China still diverges fundamentally from what is meant by judicial independence or the autonomy of law in the West. In legal cases of any importance, judges are expected to engage in detailed consultation with party officials who outrank them and supervise them at the provincial level. This is not some secret deviation from the rules but the basic norm. Officials who support this more traditionally communist approach to the use of law have won significant victories in recent years against more pro-law forces. The tone and content of the 2012 white paper differed markedly from parallel documents produced in earlier years—which suggests that the intraparty fight over how to use law is not yet over.[9]

The debate in China about the uses of law reflects an important fact about the development of the rule of law that is often forgotten or misunderstood in the West. In established legal systems, people sometimes imagine that law is a tool of the weak, used to restrain the strong. But that is not the way law comes into existence. Laws are made initially by the powerful, who agree to be constrained by legal rules in exchange for a similar agreement by those with less power. The result is a greater uniformity of conduct, greater predictability, and less effort needed to monitor and enforce what everyone in the system is doing. On top of it all, the powerful are able to legitimate their position by conforming to rules that they have set to their own advantage. If the legal rules are not to their liking, powerful actors can usually change them.[10]

Given this structure, the party could probably do more than it has to govern through law without compromising its position at the top of the Chinese state and society. But the enthusiasm for reform on the part of Western and Chinese rule-of-law advocates will continue to make the party nervous that law could be used to delegitimize it. Inherent conservatism suggests that the party will not in the foreseeable future embrace the rule of law, which could undercut the delicate principle that it stands above principles. The upshot is that in the ideological struggle around the law, the West would have to compromise significantly if it wanted to reduce conflict.

Democracy and Its Limits

Democracy is much newer than law as a broadly held Western ideal, yet compromising on democracy is even harder than on law. Many people all over the world—not only in the West—believe in the inherent right to participate in collective self-determination according to some system of majority rule. And many people certainly believe, with still greater force, that everyone must be entitled to an equal voice in how things are run: one person, one vote.

What is more, many in the West have deep faith in democratic institutions like elections and consider them to be essential to a just system of government. George W. Bush believed in elections in this absolute way.[11] Although his advisers cautioned him against the many risks of holding elections in the Arab world, Bush pushed their objections aside. Behind this was a moral commitment to self-determination. The ink-stained fingers of Iraqis casting meaningful votes for the first time in their lives were the tangible symbol of this universalist aspiration.

Yet despite the existence of this sort of quasi-religious commitment to elections, Western political thought is also ambivalent about elections—in particular, the principle of majority rule. Why should the minority always lose? Elections are an excellent technique for giving effect to the will of the majority. But to the extent that democrats want everyone to have an equal opportunity to shape outcomes, elections are structurally flawed. Everyone speaks, but only one side wins. Over time, minority participants in elections may see themselves as perpetual losers and begin to wonder whether they truly do have an equal chance. What is more, the majority will be tempted to treat the minority unjustly—and elections will provide the minority with little or no recourse.

Responding to the worry that majority rule does not work for the minority, liberalism has modified electoral democracy with a set of institutions designed to limit what the majority can do. Constitutions and courts aim to protect minority rights, effectively undercutting the principle of majority rule. It is sometimes argued that the limitations are justified in democratic terms because they serve the goal of equal opportunity. But even if this is so, the felt need to override majority rule suggests that elections themselves may simply be one tool for enabling government to make good decisions, not a moral imperative that must be applied universally.

According to this view, elections are not primarily about equality or self-determination. Rather, they do a modestly good job of ensuring government accountability. The limits of electoral accountability are painfully clear to anyone who lives in a democracy. But the absence of elections shows just how useful they can be, because accountability is very difficult without them. It was surely this accountability-oriented vision of democracy that Winston Churchill had in mind when he said that democracy is the worst system of government except for all the others.

When democracy is understood only as a technology to achieve effective, legitimate government, it becomes just one among several possible tools. If democracy is seen in this modest way, then the

United States could more easily compromise on China's undemocratic status. It would not have to commit itself with evangelical zeal to the expansion of democracy. It could cooperate with China knowing full well that this cooperation would strengthen China and through that the nondemocratic Communist Party.

Seen in historic terms, such a shift in U.S. attitudes toward the spread of democracy around the globe would represent a striking change. Since Woodrow Wilson claimed to be fighting World War I in order to make the world safe for democracy, the expansion of democratic ideals and the principles of self-determination and self-governance through elections have been important features of American public rhetoric. The ideology of the Cold War called for the ultimate democratization of the peoples under the domination of the Soviet Union, and the same rationale was heard regarding Iraq and Afghanistan. It would be politically challenging, and probably impossible, for a president of the United States to say that democracy is not the desired end goal for China.

But the reality has always been more complicated. The United States has taken as allies many nondemocratic states, from the authoritarian anticommunist dictatorships of Latin America to the authoritarian, semisocialist dictatorships and absolute religious monarchies of the Arab world. During the Cold War, alliances with nondemocratic powers were justified as necessary to serve the ultimate goal of democracy, both in the United States and elsewhere.

Since the fall of the Soviet Union, this justification has rung hollow. Today the American public seems to tolerate alliances with nondemocratic states because they are useful—and because those states are clearly subordinate to the United States. The U.S. alliance with Saudi Arabia has everything to do with maintaining the flow of inexpensive oil—just as it always has. That interest outlived the Cold War, and so it also outlived its democratic justification. No one, least of all the United States, is in the process of democratizing Saudi Arabia. But neither does Saudi Arabia represent a major international ideological threat. To the extent that radical Islam is conceived that way, Americans seem prepared to fight it.

In theory, then, the United States might conceivably tone down its rhetoric in favor of the spread of democracy and bring it in closer relation to its actual, more neutral practices. Reducing the ideological struggle with China might potentially enable a more cooperative long-term relationship between the countries. But given the size and influence of China, the United States is not going to abandon its commitment to the universality of democracy. It follows that, whether stated or not, the American ideological position will call into question the legitimacy of the Chinese government.

Human Rights

Human rights ideology is even newer than democratic ideology— and is harder still to alter in the interest of compromise. In practical terms, the U.S. government has always used human rights ideology as a tool of international politics, deployed when convenient and ignored otherwise. This reality would seem to support the contention that the United States could and should reduce its use of this rhetoric vis-à-vis China. Something similar was surely on the mind of the Obama administration when in 2009, during his first visit to China, Barack Obama remained completely silent on the question of human rights—something no president since Richard Nixon had done on a visit to the country.

The trouble with this analysis is that it ignores, ultimately, the moral status of human rights. Human rights are universal rights of humans. By definition, they apply always and everywhere and must not to be sacrificed for short-term gain. It would be wrong to accept violations of human rights to sustain the U.S. relationship with China.

It would also be unrealistic for the government of the United States to commit itself to abandoning the issue. The Chinese would know that future U.S. administrations might simply readopt the human rights criticisms. Indeed, that is exactly what the Obama administration did after a series of well-publicized defeats by the Chinese government on currency issues. One reason the Chinese government may not have taken seriously Obama's implied proffer of a reduction in human rights criticism is that it did not believe Obama could sustain such a stance over time.

Cool war conditions will affect the practice and development of human rights, as I will discuss later in more detail. For now it is sufficient to note that human rights constitute an important source of ideological conflict of the kind that will make the struggle between the United States and China into a battle of ideas—not merely a conflict of national interests.

THE CONTRADICTION OF COOL WAR

The neologism *cold war* challenged and changed the meaning of war by broadening its functional definition beyond active hostilities. *Cool war* denotes a reality that is substantially more complex. Properly understood, it should help us reformulate the very notions of war and peace, of cooperation and competition.

Extensive cooperation in economics, intense competition in geopolitics: this new situation poses extraordinary risks. China and the United States are indeed bound together in a mutual embrace of economic interdependence. They are also on a course to conflict driven by their divergent interests and ideologies. Escalating hostility might lead not only to violence but to economic disaster. Yet economic interdependence also poses unique opportunities for the peaceful resolution of conflict. What is more, it creates common interests that mitigate the impulse to domination.

There is something odd about the idea of strategic conflict and economic cooperation going on simultaneously. Trading partners are not supposed to make war on each other. Strategic opponents are not supposed to make each other richer through financing and trade.

In the cool war, the United States and China will be able to cooperate and form alliances on some important issues that interest both sides, something that was rare or impossible in the Cold War. Where they are in agreement, these powerful players will have an enormous impact on everyone else. Trade, to which I will return, is the most important example. The United States and China have a shared long-term interest in sustaining an international trade regime that facilitates continued exchange on a grand scale—and they want as many countries as possible to participate in it. Both will try to interpret existing trade agreements and negotiate new ones in accordance with their interests. They may even try to game the trade system if they can get away with it. But they agree on the existence of the system.

Not every issue will be susceptible to such agreement. On climate control, the West, which is already industrialized, seeks limitations on emissions of greenhouse gases to save the planet from overheating. China, like India, weighs climate control much less heavily. It has years of industrial development ahead and a strong desire to unify its regions through automobile travel. Its natural allies on this issue are other countries that hope to develop and that consider it outrageous for the Western countries who polluted the environment in the first place now to demand that they forgo the benefits of the same technologies that made the West rich. The new context for this policy debate is its connection to the question of global sovereignty: who is, ultimately, in charge of the earth and its temperature? Both sides want to win. Barring invention of a new technology that replaces oil, neither side can win without the other side losing.

What is more, in a highly complex world of contradiction between geopolitical and economic interests, cooperation and competition, it will be harder than ever to figure out what is in a country's national interest. Persistent disagreement is going to be a recurring reality of our new historical era. Policy decisions can reflect internal tensions between different political and economic factions as well as genuine perplexity about the wisest thing to do.

The geopolitical interests of the United States and China clash. In realist terms, they are going to be at war. Yet the war status between the two countries falls well short of requiring actual violence. During the Cold War, what stopped the United States and the Soviet Union from fighting directly with each other was the threat of mutually assured nuclear destruction. Although the Chinese nuclear arsenal today is far less powerful than was the Soviet Union's, the dangers of nuclear conflict are part of what keeps the United States and China from direct confrontation. In this limited sense, cool war has an important similarity to cold war.

Economic cooperation, moreover, does not suffice to move relations between the United States and China definitively into the column of peace. Close economic ties make fighting less likely but do not preclude the possibility of warfare. Economic cooperation cannot eliminate geostrategic conflict because it cannot be wholly separated from the context of warfare and force.

The problem would exist even for perfectly rational states that acted only according to their idealized interests. Rational states can make war when they have misjudged their enemies' military capacities. Such states may similarly be unable to judge the economic costs of warfare correctly. It follows that rational, interdependent states could nevertheless find themselves at war.[1]

The problem exists more strongly still in our imperfect world, where unreason often prevails over rational interests. We may perhaps be wiser than our ancestors, but we cannot claim to have conquered unreasonable enthusiasm or illogical fear, as the behavior of financial markets shows. Acting on incomplete information, people make mistakes. Acting on sentiment, we sometimes do the opposite of what we would do when we are thinking calmly. Given how irrationally we humans can behave, the fact of economic interdependence is unlikely to make war obsolete.

Some readers might balk at the use of the term *war* to describe a situation in which the struggle for geopolitical preeminence exists alongside simultaneous economic cooperation. They might even fear that the word itself engenders hostility. My intention is otherwise. Speaking of a cool war is aimed at reducing hostility, not encouraging it. Calling things by their proper names is the first step to clear thinking. And clear thinking is the first step to avoiding conflict.

In what follows, I want to explore the mechanisms of the cool war and its far-reaching consequences. The operation of the U.S. system of government, with all its virtues and defects, is highly important to making sense of the coming historical era. But it is at present relatively stable and well understood by experts and laypeople around the word. In contrast, the operation, aspirations, and dynamics of the Chinese system of government are very much under development—and they are poorly understood everywhere, including perhaps even within China itself. I do not claim to offer an exhaustive account. But without offering an interpretation of how China is governed, we cannot envision the outcomes of cool war. It is thus to the subject of the internal governance of China that I now turn.

PART TWO

THE SOURCES OF CHINESE CONDUCT

CHAPTER FOUR

A GLIMPSE INTO THE NEW CHINA

The U.S. consulate in the city of Chengdu is a drab, midlevel affair tucked behind a stucco-covered wall and a halfhearted spray of barbed wire. But on February 6, 2012, what happened there was anything but dull. The chief of police and vice mayor of the neighboring city of Chongqing, one of the most important cities in all of China, came in without an appointment and asked for asylum.

Wang Lijun wasn't an ordinary police chief. Having spearheaded major investigations against the powerful triad mafia of Chongqing, he was the best-known anticorruption cop in the country. Under the direction of Bo Xilai, the head of the municipality and a member of the national Politburo, Wang had deployed the Chongqing police as a formidable weapon against organized crime. More than two thousand people had been arrested in the previous three years.

Wang's methods were not gentle. Arbitrary arrests, interrogation, and even torture were used in the effort to root out corruption from what was seen as one of the most corrupt places in the country. But the anticorruption campaign seemed to be working. Partly on the strength of these efforts, Bo Xilai had become one of the most famous and popular figures in Chinese national politics.

Wang Lijun knew perfectly well that, as a high-ranking police official, he could not be granted asylum without causing a major international scandal. He had to have something pretty extraordinary to trade if he were to have any chance of not being turned over to the Chinese government. Behind closed doors, Wang demanded to see the highest-ranking official he could. Then he delivered his bombshell. He told the American diplomats that Bo Xilai's wife had murdered a shadowy British businessman named Neil Heywood. The motive was (and remains) hazy, but apparently Heywood had set up a large, illegal land deal abroad for Bo's wife, and when it fell through, continued to blackmail her for his fee.[1]

The diplomats at the consulate telephoned Ambassador Gary Locke in Beijing. If they had time, they surely tried to check Wang's story. They would have found that Neil Heywood was indeed a forty-one-year-old British national who had made his living connecting Western firms with Chinese government officials. He did have a business relationship with Gu Kailai, Bo's wife.

On November 14, 2011, Heywood had checked in to the Lucky Holiday Hotel in the Nan'an district of Chongqing. Some twenty-six hours later, he was found dead in his hotel room. The apparent cause of death was alcohol poisoning. Heywood's wife traveled from their home in Beijing to Chongqing, and with her agreement, Heywood's body was cremated. There was no autopsy.

Wang's revelation threatened to precipitate a crisis. What was to be done with a police chief who claimed that his life was in danger as a result of his own murder investigation? Several days earlier, Wang had been demoted from his official job as head of public security. It was rumored that he might have implicated Bo on corruption charges before an official Communist Party inquiry. Were his allegations now to be taken seriously? What were the political implications of whatever would happen next?

Behind these questions lay another fascinating story: the meteoric political career of Bo Xilai, the husband of the accused—one of the fastest-rising men in the new China. Bo's background, his career trajectory, and the troubles he engendered and encountered are an invaluable lens for understanding China's governing elite and how it runs the country. As it turns out, the murder of Neil Heywood was not merely a representative event of the new cool war era but an opportunity to reveal the fast-changing rules of the game by which that war will be conducted.

The Rise of Bo Xilai

Bo Xilai's story begins properly not with his birth in 1949 but a quarter century before that, in 1925, when his father, Bo Yibo, then a teenager, joined the Chinese Communist Party. Bo the father rose within the party, joined Mao for part of the legendary Long March, and would, in the year of his son's birth, emerge as a senior party official and minister of finance in Mao's earliest government. He later served as head of the state planning commission during the Great Leap Forward, Mao's ill-starred economic initiative that cost the lives of 30 million rural Chinese.

Long a member of the Politburo, the powerful twenty-five-member group that sits atop the Communist Party, Bo senior was purged at the beginning of the Cultural Revolution. But in its aftermath, through his close alliance with Deng Xiaoping—the father of the Chinese reform movement and the new de facto leader after Mao's death—Bo regained his status as a major figure. He was one of the "eight immortals," key leaders who made decisions with Deng as China transformed into a quasi-capitalist economy or, as the system is officially called, "socialism with Chinese characteristics."

Bo the son was therefore born into communist royalty. In the parlance of contemporary China, he is a "princeling": the offspring of a powerful and important government official who came out of the original communist leadership. Being a princeling affords enormous advantages for a political or business career in China today. Bo exploited all of them.

In the Chinese communist system, relationships are everything. The formal system for choosing members of the Communist Party, then for selecting government officials from among their ranks, was adopted by the Chinese communists from the Soviet method devised by Lenin. The *nomenklatura* system, as the Soviets called it, empowers committees of party members to choose candidates for advancement and appointment from lists of names. The way a person navigates a career through party advancement depends on how he or she is judged and valued by the members of the relevant committees.

As a result, the entire Chinese Communist Party operates through a web of personal networks. If you start from scratch, with only your own connections, it may require years of hard work, accomplishment, and relationship building to attach yourself to existing networks and eventually develop your own. If, however, you inherit your father's powerful network, you start pretty close to the top. Your name is known, and your reputation can follow.

Bo Xilai began his career in the central party apparatus in Beijing, aided by his father, who remained an important and influential figure until his death in 2007. But Bo did not rest solely on his father's connections. In 1984, following the career path of the ancient Chinese bureaucratic elites, he accepted a position in the provinces. Starting as a deputy party secretary of the Dalian Economic and Technological Development Zone in China's far northeast, Bo began to rise on his own. He became mayor and eventually party secretary of Dalian. In all, he spent seventeen years out of Beijing.

During Bo's years in Dalian, the city became a model of the new Chinese path. Its economy flourished. Major infrastructure projects, including a superhighway, changed the landscape. Bo expanded public space in Dalian, moving the urban population into the suburbs to make room for parks and boulevards. He combined capitalist-oriented economic development with a significant dose of populism and a taste for publicity. By the end of his tenure, people were calling the formerly sleepy Dalian "the Hong Kong of the North." Bo had developed a strategy of his own for success within the party—and a reputation to go with it.

Now it was time for Bo to move up in the world. With his father pushing hard for him, he sought membership in the Central Committee at the 1997 Communist Party Congress. The plan fell short, and Bo failed to get the coveted seat. But Bo's father had loyally supported President Jiang Zemin for years, helping him to take power in the aftermath of the Tiananmen Square protests. When the governorship of Liaoning opened up in 2001 as the result of a corruption scandal, Jiang helped make sure that Bo got it. As the governorship came with a seat on the Central Committee, the father-and-son team had achieved their goal. By 2002, when the next party congress took place according to the five-year cycle, Bo was perceived as a leading candidate for the so-called fifth generation of leaders who would eventually run the country from 2012 onward.

That still left a decade of maneuvering. Bo spent the first five years of it as minister of commerce, learning Beijing politics and international trade. In 2007, at the next party congress, Bo hoped to become vice premier. Instead he got a much harder job, one that carried publicly measurable risks of failure. He became party chief and mayor of the municipality of Chongqing, one of four cities in China so important that they have the status of independent provinces.

Chongqing was already an economic success. But it was plagued by pollution and other environmental difficulties caused by the ill-conceived Three Gorges Dam project along the Yangtze River upstream from the city. Then there was the problem of corruption. Chongqing boasted the most aggressive and powerful mafia of any Chinese city. The triads were large, powerful, and vicious—and government officials were known to be in cahoots with them.

Faced with these formidable challenges, Bo shone. Serious anticorruption efforts would require police reform, so Bo brought in Wang Lijun, who had been his chief of police during his brief term as governor of Liaoning. No one was spared in the investigations and arrests that followed, including municipal officials with close ties to previous Chongqing-area party leaders. Wary of derailing his career ambitions by frightening corrupt officials elsewhere, Bo tried not to state publicly that his anticorruption campaign was a model for the whole country. But the thought was inevitable. The international press began to call Bo a "rock star" of Chinese national politics.

As he had done during his long years in Dalian, Bo did not neglect the symbolic, populist aspects of governance. He built or commissioned highly visible public projects, like a soaring, ship-inspired six-skyscraper complex at the confluence of the Yangtze and Jialing rivers. And he began, in a limited way, to revive some of Mao's rhetoric and emphasis on the poor, albeit without a return to classically Maoist policies. He built low-income housing in the city in addition to expensive luxury towers. He emphasized the need to distribute wealth to all—not merely to grow the economic pie, but to divide it up fairly. In terms of Chinese politics, this put Bo on the left, in favor of maintaining state control and ownership and sharing the benefits of new wealth.

The success of Bo's anticorruption campaign and the resonance in some parts of Chinese society of his left rhetoric pushed him to the very forefront of Chinese politics. The sought-for prize this time was membership in the Standing Committee of the Politburo of the Central Committee of the Communist Party, seven of whose members would be replaced in the fall of 2012. This body was the sine qua non of Chinese politics—the very pinnacle of power in the country. From among its members would come the new president and premier.

Although it is impossible for outsiders to track with any confidence the ins and outs of the complex negotiations that create the membership of the Politburo Standing Committee, most observers believed Bo had a serious shot at making it. He had begun with strong connections and then had done everything right. He was famous, and famously self-promoting. No one knew for sure what role he would get, but it was difficult to imagine him being excluded from the Standing Committee altogether—until Wang Lijun, Bo's handpicked police chief, walked into the consulate general accusing Bo's wife of murder.

Things Fall Apart

The first task that faced the consulate, the embassy, and Washington was to figure out what to do with Wang. Even when two countries are on relatively good terms, it can be diplomatically disastrous for a consulate or embassy in one country to get into the habit of granting asylum to citizens of that state. The difficulty is exaggerated when those countries are, like the United States and China, at odds over important issues of policy and ideology. Legally, a diplomatic post is a little enclave of the foreign country. In reality, its status is very much that of a guest. To do their jobs, diplomats must cultivate positive relations with the host government. Protecting the host government's citizens from the host government is a good way to wear out your welcome fast.

To make matters worse, the United States and China have a history of struggle over Chinese citizens seeking refuge in U.S. diplomatic posts. At the time of the Tiananmen protests in 1989, a Chinese human rights activist and physicist, Fang Lizhi, had been sheltered in the U.S. embassy in Beijing. The result was a major diplomatic standoff that lasted a full year. It took up enormous amounts of American and Chinese diplomatic energy until it was resolved by Fang issuing a formal "confession"—which he later retracted after being allowed to leave the country.

Against this background, the Obama administration decided to avoid another standoff. Wang Lijun was not a human rights activist but a policeman who had himself been accused of overzealousness to the point of violating human rights. The Americans negotiated a fast solution: Wang would be turned over to the authorities in Beijing. Thus the United States would not be handing him over to Bo, who he alleged was pursuing him. At the same time, the United States would be acting creditably vis-à-vis the Chinese government. Although Congress immediately initiated an inquiry into how and why the decision was taken, no other result was really politically possible. Indeed, given Wang's level of government experience, it is conceivable that this was all he expected. Perhaps his only goal in going to the consulate was to assure that he would not die in a hotel bed like Neil Heywood.

The United States would have been pleased to pretend the whole affair had never happened, but that turned out to be impossible. Already on February 4, two days before he entered the consulate but after he lost the job as police chief, Wang's name had been blocked by the Chinese government's Internet firewall. On February 8, however, the government censors removed the block. The fact of Wang's strange adventure, though not yet what he had said to the Americans, was now public knowledge. Wang was taken back to Beijing in custody. The public fall of Bo Xilai had begun.

Bo's political enemies began to whisper that "the Wang Lijun incident" would harm Bo's chances of becoming a member of the Politburo Standing Committee. They emphasized the embarrassment of a Chinese government official presenting himself to the U.S. consulate. For Wang to have gone outside the system was a national humiliation. Critics also suggested, plausibly enough, that the incident cast doubt on the value of Bo's entire anticorruption campaign.

In March, a month after the incident, the National People's Congress met in Beijing. Bo was at first conspicuously absent. Then he gave a press conference at which he defended himself and his record—an unusual example of a Communist Party official using the foreign and local media to press his case with his senior party colleagues. By the end of a week, however, those colleagues had decided his political fate. Bo was relieved of his position as Chongqing party secretary and mayor on May 15, 2012.

Had this been the end of the affair, it would still have mattered enormously by revealing to the outside world the structure of contemporary Chinese politics within the Communist Party. But it was not over. The Bo Xilai situation had gotten beyond Wang Lijun and his visit to the consulate. It was now about the nature of party rule—and what could be done to improve it.

Finding itself in the crosshairs, the party moved quickly to deal with the scandal. In the months that followed, a formal criminal investigation of Bo's wife, Gu Kailai, began. Gu was pressured to plead guilty to murder. In her unconvincing confession, she claimed that Heywood had threatened her son, who was living abroad, and that she had killed Heywood to protect him. There was no official mention of corruption in the charges against her or in her confession, and Gu's death sentence was suspended.

Then charges were filed against the police chief, Wang Lijun, for covering up the murder and for bribery—presumably in connection with the cover-up. No mention of broader corruption was made. After a secret and brief trial, Wang pleaded guilty, avoiding the death penalty.[2]

In the denouement, Bo Xilai was expelled from the party so that he too could stand trial. His alleged crimes were involvement in the Heywood murder, alleged sexual relationships with several women—formally illegal under Chinese law—and other unspecified abuses of power.

None of these allegations or trials was accompanied by public fact finding. But sufficient evidence was leaked or rumored to suggest the general outline of the events in question. And what this tentative evidence reveals is highly significant.

The central character in the affair was, it would seem, Gu Kailai herself. Bo's second wife, Gu is a princeling in her own right. Her father was a high-ranking general and old-line communist. Like Bo and many senior leaders of the fifth generation, she was trained in law and international affairs at Beijing University, one of the most prestigious educational institutions in the country.[3] She founded a law firm of her own and ensured that her son, Bo Guagua, would study at Harrow, Oxford, and Harvard.

Gu's involvement in Bo's business affairs afforded the basis for her relationship with Neil Heywood. Heywood seems to have met Bo and Gu through their connections to Dalian, which is where Heywood's wife, a Chinese national, was born. Their connections were personal as well as professional. Heywood, an old Harrovian, most likely played a role in enabling Bo Guagua to go to the famed British public school.

Rumor inevitably suggested a romantic connection between Gu and Heywood, but there seems to be no evidence for this claim. It was also rumored that Heywood was a British spy. Britain's foreign secretary denied that Heywood had worked for the British government in any capacity, a denial that presumably convinced no one who already believed the rumor. What does seem likely is that conflict arose between Gu and Heywood over a business deal outside China. Heywood apparently sought more payment for his role than Gu wanted to provide, and backed up his demands with some threat that furnished the motive for his murder by poison. The murder, in turn, was covered up by the police. An otherwise healthy forty-one-year-old man does not ordinarily die of alcohol poisoning alone in his hotel room. Wang Lijun, the chief of police, was complicit in the cover-up.

What It All Means

The spectacular nature of these events nevertheless seemed utterly unsurprising to many Chinese observers. The entire tale confirmed several widely held beliefs. For one, senior Chinese Communist Party officials engage in corruption—a perception widely shared throughout the country. For another, not only officials but their family members act as though immune from law—another frequently heard complaint, one substantiated by notorious examples. Still another: China has a hereditary elite made up of princelings who enjoy enormous advantages in the complex Chinese political system. And above it all, hypocrisy looms. Bo Xilai, the poster child for anticorruption, was harboring corruption in his own home— corruption so deep that it led to murder.

Seen from the outside, these conclusions would appear to present major challenges to the legitimacy of the Communist Party as the governing force in China. The foreign press largely presented the story of Bo and Gu in these terms. The relative speed with which the loose ends were tied up, in advance of the party congress in late 2012, lends support to this interpretation.

But this is too simplistic a view of the Bo Xilai affair and the way the government and party handled it. No doubt the public confirmation of negative stereotypes about the party was threatening to its legitimacy. Yet the affair also represented an enormous opportunity for the party: an opportunity to produce a narrative that would focus not on the rise of Bo Xilai but on his fall. This counternarrative reveals much about the structure of the new model of governance that the Communist Party of China is gradually and experimentally trying to create.

The counternarrative begins with the membership of the Chinese governing elite. True, Bo and Gu were model princelings, blessed with the privilege of their parents' deep and powerful party networks. But not every member of the Chinese elite is a princeling. Many are meritocrats, people who have advanced by fulfilling the party's chosen criteria of intelligence, competence, loyalty, and networking skill. The leadership of the Communist Party is made up of meritocrats *and* princelings. And despite their head start over pure meritocrats, those princelings must still display merit to advance. Bo himself had considerable merit, measured by Chinese standards.

More important still, Bo's story is not only about a princeling advancing in politics with his father's assistance, but how he never quite made it into the highest echelon of power—the Politburo Standing Committee. His story is about how political transitions happen in China. The Chinese leadership is a self-replacing, self-vetting, and self-analyzing elite. When the party's senior leadership met in March 2012, preparing for the crucial decisions that would be made and announced in November, they purged Bo. They did not allow him to remain in their midst, much less remain in the mix for promotion. Instead, they ended his career.

Many Chinese observers saw the distancing and eventual expulsion of Bo as an artifact of partisan politics—a defeat for his leftist policies and for other members of his network. This was certainly part of the story. At the same time, however, the party, by making this decision, also intended to send a second message: that China's leaders are chosen by a rational and wise process. Throwing out a bad apple may cause worry about whether the rest of the barrel is rotten, but the fact that the apple has been thrown out signals that the rest of the barrel is now relatively safe. No one is exempt from being made an example.

Finally, Bo's fall could be seen as a victory for public accountability. Yes, Gu was corrupt, and Bo probably was, too. But they were caught—and the government responded to the resulting public outrage. Yes, Gu almost got away with murder. But she didn't—and she was punished for it. The Chinese government could have suppressed the story, or at least restricted the flow of information over the Internet and elsewhere. Great scandals have been suppressed before in China's history. But instead the government allowed a limited degree of public discourse around the whole affair.

Following what has become a tentative pattern when it comes to public concerns, including corruption, the government did not seek total or immediate suppression of the topic. The speech norm that has emerged in the age of the Internet allows for time-limited discussion—followed by a rapid and sharp government response to the problem at hand. Although the discussion is typically shut down, by the time this happens, the public has had the opportunity to conclude that its concerns are being addressed. This is not free speech in the Western sense. But it produces a version of government accountability.

Finally, Bo's eventual fall can be described as a victory for effective anticorruption. Despite Bo's anticorruption credentials, because he and Gu were corrupt themselves, their efforts unwittingly swept them up in the process. Corruption, like murder, will out. The process of cleaning up China's leadership is therefore moving forward.

The alternative narrative of the fall of Bo Xilai captures all the major elements of the new model of governance that the Chinese Communist Party is gradually and experimentally developing. Here we can see the structure of the elite that comprises the governing class in China, and the ways that elite structures political transitions. We can also glimpse the effort to create an accountable, responsive government that listens to its citizens and fights corruption. This second part of the book is devoted to the elements of that model. It differs strikingly from the model of liberal democracy—but it also differs from dictatorship.

The new model tries to create a governing elite that is renewed by the fresh blood of meritocrats while still keeping the elite committed to the system across the generations. This is the very essence of the liberal democratic model of elite governance, at least in the case of the United States. Anyone can grow up to be president of the United States—as Bill Clinton and Barack Obama can testify. But it helps to be born to the ruling class, as George H. W. Bush and George W. Bush can both attest. The United States draws its ruling elites both from merit and from heredity—and so today does China.

Democracy solves the problem of political transitions through elections. When modern democracy was new, skeptics insisted that only royal heredity could create the kind of regular political transitions necessary to establish continuity over time and hence a stable environment for politics and investment alike. The skeptics were wrong. Democracy, when it works, has turned out to be spectacularly good at facilitating the shift in power from one faction or party to another.

In general, the Chinese Communist Party eschews elections.[4] But nor does it embrace dictatorship, which is poorly suited to peaceful transition. Rather, through its structure of five-year party conferences and ten-year generational shifts, the party is trying to create regularized, smooth, institutionalized power transitions. The process is very complicated—as are elections. To survive, a political system must solve the transition problem. China has in place a model that may be able to stand the test of time.

Any successful, lasting government must also provide accountability if it does not want the public to give up on it altogether. Here democracy has proven especially brilliant. To be accountable, monarchs had to demonstrate that they were listening to their subjects' concerns. In a democracy, elections operate as a kind of magic bullet. The citizens of a democratic state believe there is accountability because they get to vote for their representatives. Whether this is true or not is debatable. It depends on the nature of the voting system (and its funding), who chooses the candidates, the number of voters per district, and many other factors. But from the standpoint of democracy as a system, none of this matters. Democracy accepts accountability as a dogma.

China's new model of governance cannot derive accountability from national elections. It has to look elsewhere, to the experiences of individuals who want their voices heard by relevant government officials. Totalitarian dictatorship generally cannot afford to allow public criticism. By contrast, in China, limited public criticism exists. And it is permitted because, within those limits, it can be beneficial.[5]

Public comment through the Internet, and even actual old-fashioned protests in the streets, function in the new Chinese model as a way for the government to obtain information about what the public believes and wants. Different parts of the government can then decide how serious and widespread these concerns may be and act accordingly. By allowing people to complain—and by allowing other people to know that those people are complaining— the government creates conditions for accountability.

The possibility of accountability is not the same as providing incentives to complain. Protesters may be punished, and those who complain may be silenced. What is more, the party's eventual response, even when it is what the protesters sought, may look grudging to outside observers because it comes only after public protest. But what matters for accountability is that the squeaky wheel gets the grease. If I complain about something the government is doing and then that thing is changed, the government has acted accountably. It has listened to me, even if I am punished for complaining in the first place.

A mixed or permeable elite; regular transitions; accountable government; and the emerging, if incomplete, battle against corruption: these are the core elements of China's new governance model. Taken together, they represent an attempt to create a durable and legitimate governing structure. Allowing for differences of approach and opinion, the Chinese leadership has a common incentive to see this model succeed. And this incentive in turn will structure the cool war.

CHAPTER FIVE

CHINA'S PERMEABLE ELITE

On September 5, 2012, China's vice president missed a meeting. That in itself would not have been terribly odd. But the meeting was with U.S. secretary of state Hillary Clinton, and the vice president, Xi Jinping, was the man slated to become general secretary of the Communist Party by the end of the year and president by spring. Xi certainly had no objection to meeting U.S. officials. Earlier in 2012, he had spoken to Barack Obama in the Oval Office as part of an extended five-day getting-to-know-you visit to the United States. Clinton's staff was mystified but said nothing.

Then things got stranger still. For the next two weeks, the fifty-nine-year-old Xi did not appear in public at all. The foreign news media were abuzz with rumors. Xi had hurt his back playing sports. He had suffered a slight heart attack. A frustrated general had tried to assassinate him by hitting him with a car. Apparently seeking to dampen concern, the Chinese media ran a photo of the vice president—taken September 1, the last time he had appeared in public. After that, both government sources and the Chinese media fell silent.

What was going on? Had the second most powerful man in

China somehow been purged? If so, what would that mean for the carefully staged, closely watched transition of power scheduled for the fall? Enormous effort had gone into making this process look as smooth as possible. Now, quite suddenly, it seemed in danger of blowing up.

Transitions

China is an authoritarian state—but it is not a dictatorship. In a dictatorship, a single, dominant figure gathers legitimacy to the point where he can make the most important decisions for the country entirely on his own. China arguably functioned as a dictatorship under Mao Zedong. Yet it has not done so for several rounds of government stretching back into the 1980s.[1]

Here the most astonishing fact about how China is now governed comes into play: every ten years, starting in 1992, continuing in 2002, and most recently in 2012, the Chinese Communist Party has retired its most senior group of leaders and replaced them with another group roughly ten years younger.

The fact is so striking that it bears repetition: in a regular pattern, China's leaders voluntarily retire and are replaced by younger men (so far it is almost all men). In November 2012, as on previous occasions, the new Politburo and Politburo Standing Committee were announced as scheduled. Xi Jinping was at the head of it, a fact determined as early as 2010 through consultation within the party and the decisive influence of senior officials. That all this would take place seemed as certain and predictable as the fact that the U.S. presidential election would happen the same year.[2]

Regular, planned transitions almost never happen in dictatorships. Dictators tend to die in office. Their fondest wish is usually to pass their position on to their children, but this aspiration is rarely fulfilled. (North Korea is one of the few examples where this has happened successfully in the modern world.)

Voluntary retirement and generational transition at the top were not always the norm in communist China. Mao rose from a group of leaders to a position of preeminence, fell from power, and reemerged at the time of the Cultural Revolution. Deng Xiaoping, whose importance for the creation of contemporary China cannot be overstated, stayed in power until he was extremely old, although he may be credited with initiating the norm of retirement.

Today, however, China has seen not just one or two but three successful voluntary transitions. They occurred on time, as scheduled. Retiring figures retained some influence but not formal authority. No leader demanded to keep his position or his de facto power. The public was able to speculate in advance on which leaders would emerge.

The process was not transparent. China's most senior leaders do not stand for public election. They rise to the top of the Communist Party through a lengthy, complex series of bureaucratic steps that results in their selection from their generational cohort through consensus. That consensus is intensely political. Even experts on the Communist Party have trouble explaining exactly how much of promotion is related to networks of friendships and patronage and how much to successful fulfillment of government or party jobs. It is possible that party members themselves would not be able to articulate such a complex series of social processes fully.[3]

Westerners are unaccustomed to the idea of such complex social processes being used to select government officials. They expect a rule that can be stated simply: The king's eldest son inherits. The candidate with the most votes wins. The prime minister appoints her cabinet. But Western institutions, too, often involve complex consensus. Candidates for national office in the United States are no longer selected in smoke-filled rooms, yet much political deal making still happens behind closed doors. Party donors can back a single candidate without an electoral process. Then they can fund that candidate so heavily that others withdraw from the race.

It is therefore a mistake for Westerners to treat the Chinese process of selecting officials—with its anonymity, its networking, and its secrecy—as utterly unfamiliar. In fact, selection of the elite classes in China and the United States has more in common than is generally believed. To understand how the cool war will proceed, we need to get behind the opacity of the Chinese approach to selecting leaders. Understanding the structure of the selection, and how it combines self-made men with hereditary elites, will shed light on the leaders' incentives. That in turn will help us understand what China's leaders are likely to do once in power.

The Life and Death of an Elite

What, really, is a ruling elite? To last more than a single generation, every system of government needs to have some mechanism for the transition of power from one leader or set of leaders to another. Transitions run smoothly when all the participants believe that the process in some way serves their interests, at least enough to reduce their incentive to interfere with it. The danger to regular transition is revolution—defined as a fundamental change in how leaders are selected.

Remarkably enough, in the history of political thought, there are really only two major strategies for selecting the people who would rule a given society or state. One is family. The connections between human beings that are formed on the basis of kinship are powerful and durable. Family structures inherently cross generations, which makes them natural candidates for creating political institutions that endure.[4] As the history of monarchy has proved countless times, heredity does little to ensure that the next generation of rulers will be talented or capable. But regression to the mean is just the flip side of the benefits that come with the designation of a predictable heir.

A further great advantage of family as a method for the selection of elites is that it provides an incentive for those elites to invest in the system and remain committed to it across generations. Elites who expect their children to become elites will want to keep the system functioning well so that they can pass it on. The English lord whose manor is entailed to his eldest son wants the walls to be sturdy and the estate to be debt-free. By contrast, a dictator who believes he cannot transfer power to his children successfully will not have the same investment in the country. Like the kleptocrat Mobuto Sese Seko of Zaire, he will steal the country's wealth, either to pass it to his children or for personal gratification.

The alternative to selection by family is selection by merit. *Merit* is by definition an open-ended term: merit is whatever the system considers worthy. Some cultures favor bravery, others charisma, still others social intelligence or even analytical skill. Some may prefer height, or honor as they understand it, or a luxuriant head of hair. All of these, even those that might sound silly, come under the heading of merit for our purposes. Each system can define merit for itself, whether consciously or unconsciously. *Merit* is simply the word we use to denote whatever principle of selection the system is in fact using to choose leaders. Democracy, for example, is a form of merit-based selection. Even if the voters do not consciously choose the person who is smartest, bravest, or most honest, they are choosing the person who they think has the most qualities that will enable him or her to lead well.

The tremendous advantage of meritocracy is that it brings talented and ambitious people to positions of leadership. Instead of relying upon the luck of the genetic draw, leaders are those with the best capacity to lead, at least as understood by participants in the system. Once they have access to positions of leadership, the members of the new elite have an incentive to succeed in their jobs—in order to keep them.

Meritocracy therefore is an excellent system for avoiding revolution. In order to advance, those with the greatest talent and capacity to lead others will commit themselves to rising within the system. It is much easier to take over a system of government by following the rules than by creating a revolution, which is risky and costly. Meritocrats are smart enough to know that.

The drawback of merit selection is corruption. Elites cannot be sure their own children will make it past the bar and become elites themselves. If they cannot pass on power, they will pass on wealth to the next generation—by robbing the system that they lead. Such corruption can destroy the meritocratic order that unwittingly created it. In this limited sense, meritocrats can be a bit like dictators.

Toward a Permeable Elite

Given the disadvantages of both family- and merit-based selection, one effective solution to the problem of selecting rulers is to combine them both into an elite that is partly entrenched by family but also permeable to those with merit. Including family gives elites a reason to keep the system strong. Meanwhile, allowing those with merit to become elites distracts them from becoming frustrated by their exclusion from power and making revolution. Once meritocratic elites come to power, they can advance the interests of their children by becoming part of the established, family-based elite. That gives them the same intergenerational incentive already enjoyed by the old elites.

A permeable elite system is much more durable than a system of either family heredity or pure meritocracy. The most skilled potential leaders, who are often also the most likely potential revolutionaries, are continually feeding the system with new talent. They commit themselves to the system in the hopes of furthering the interests of their children, who in turn can become members of the hereditary elite. In the United States, the children of ruling elites are given the advantages of education, wealth, and name, then left to fend for themselves. They must make affirmative efforts to participate in the structures of government, and they must show at least some talent in this direction to succeed. George W. Bush and Jeb Bush are examples of this. (Bill and Hillary Clinton and Barack and Michelle Obama are all meritocrats, but their children are hereditary elites.)

One key to sustaining the system is that candidates with merit must always have a realistic chance to enter the elite. If the system becomes too crowded with hereditary elites who then take steps to exclude talented people trying to get in, the system runs the risk of conflict and enters a classic revolutionary situation. Iran before 1979 offers a famous example. The Shah of Iran, like his father, encouraged the emergence of a new merit-based elite by sending smart young people abroad for graduate training. But on their return to Iran, members of this elite-in-the-making were not rewarded with sufficient job opportunities and social mobility. They became frustrated and restless, and their support for the regime weakened. Some became communists, and some became Islamists. This revolutionary vanguard fueled the Iranian revolution in its first phase.

One way to ensure a place in the elite for talented rising meritocrats is to keep making the elite bigger. If the economy is growing fast, the strategy of expanding the elite can work for long periods of time. But no elite can be expanded without limit. It is always necessary to cull some of the members of the hereditary elite in order to make room for new talent. If the culling process is too overt, it runs the risk of reducing elites' incentive to stay committed to the system across generations. The ideal method of culling is to make the possibility of losing one's status relatively remote in likelihood or time.

In the United States, loss of family status within the ruling elite is not formalized at all. George W. and Jeb Bush's brothers Neil and Marvin are simply prosperous businessmen, and their sister, Dorothy, is a housewife in Maryland. Over generations, members of the American hereditary elite can continue to maintain their positions, or they can gradually slip into the mainstream of society.

The Communist Party as a Permeable Elite

Although the fact has not been widely recognized in the West, China's ruling class today is a permeable elite. With 75 million members, the Communist Party is too large to constitute an elite unto itself, even in a country of 1.4 billion. The ruling elite has, however, been extremely effective in choosing its members from within the party. Party membership is therefore the first cut along the way to achieving elite political status.

Close observers sometimes claim that China is in fact run by some three to four hundred very senior Communist Party members. If so, these senior leaders operate within broader networks that could easily be described as China's governing elite. This larger elite may number several hundred thousand people.[5] This is a completely manageable size for an elite network and one probably adequate for running even such a large country.

The background to China's permeable elite comes from the communist theory of revolution. Although Marx developed a theory of revolution by the workers, communism as a practical political movement always acknowledged that the workers were unlikely to rise on their own. They need leadership—and the technical name for those who lead the public to revolution is the vanguard. The revolutionary vanguard was always understood to be composed of extraordinary people. Its members had to be possessed of special vision, special talents, and special willingness to sacrifice. The vanguard also had a special organizational form. Its name was—and is—the Communist Party. Lenin perfected the theory of the Communist Party as a vanguard that would lead a permanent revolution to transform society.[6]

The Chinese Communist Party today remains based upon Lenin's basic design. Its members are tested not only for their ideological commitment but also for their capacity to lead and to perform as a team. And one of the party's most important functions is to select its own membership. As a result, the Communist Party has a highly sophisticated understanding of what it is seeking. Its members have all thought hard about what a revolutionary vanguard looks like, and who is best qualified to belong to it.

They aim, among other things, to find the people in the society who have the greatest likelihood of becoming revolutionaries and stop them from making a revolution against the party. One crude way to do that is to find potential challengers and suppress them by the threat of arrest, imprisonment, or execution. But there is a far better way to avoid revolution: identify those most likely to become revolutionaries and enlist them on behalf of the status quo. A permeable elite structure is an excellent way to make this happen.

The *nomenklatura* system for choosing members of the Communist Party, then for selecting government officials from among their ranks, relies on committees of party members to choose candidates for advancement and appointment from lists of names. In its basic structure, this is a method of merit-based choice. But the ability to rise within a *nomenklatura* system depends most fundamentally on one's capacity to form relationships with the people who are doing the choosing. The simplest such relationship is direct patronage from one committee member to one person being selected. To acquire one patron is to acquire his or her patrons in a vertical line as far toward the top as the patronage reaches. Even more important, one acquires with the patron the various horizontal relationships that the patron has with others at the same level of party membership and authority. A rising party member attaches herself to one and eventually multiple networks, then uses the ties she has formed as her constant reference point and route to power.

In any complex network of power that crosses multiple generations, family connections almost inevitably enter the picture. Networks are built on relationships, and the family relationship is underscored by both nature and culture. Not only will the child of a relatively senior party member know how the system works, which is especially valuable in an opaque system without written rules; he will also inherit actual relationships with the members of his parents' network. The effect will be especially strong when Confucianism prevails, as it now does, over the dynamics of rebellion against parents that appeared in China during the Cultural Revolution. As senior network members themselves have children who enter the party, it will be natural for them to form networks with each other.

By contrast, someone who enters the party with no family connections starts from zero. She must find a patron and expand from there. In competition with the child of a senior party member, she must make up lost ground. She may have the advantage in talent, energy, or leadership potential—but she will have to expend her energy in getting noticed and building a network, and so these advantages will certainly be less pronounced than they would be if she and a member of the hereditary elite were starting on a level playing field.

Over time, it is easy to see that hereditary party members will have interests in common with other hereditary party members. As a result, new party members who do not consider themselves part of the hereditary elite will have the incentive to align themselves with each other—to form networks of merit rather than family connections. From this scenario, factions form.

Parties Within the Party

Sure enough, when one looks at the Communist Party of China today, the most visible fault line is between the princelings and those who have risen within the party by merit, many of them through the Communist Youth League. Each group has come to power by a different method, and each therefore has an interest in maximizing its power under that method. In some sense, the divide is one that Marxist analysis might call "class-based": it is derived from the way each has generated its position of power in the society.

China faces large ideological questions—but the princelings and the meritocrats do not necessarily divide along ideological lines. Conservatives, who are called the left in China because what they seek to conserve is some form of traditional communism, are skeptical of too much market reform and fear too much free speech. Like good followers of Edmund Burke (albeit communist ones), they believe that gradualism is the key to successful evolution, and that rapid change can unleash revolution with potentially disastrous consequences.

On the side of faster reform—which in China is called the right, because it wants to move in the direction of markets—are those who believe China's tremendous growth has come from its willingness to change the old ways. The right within the Communist Party is just as devoted to the rule of the party as the left is. But it conceptualizes the role of the party as a change agent. Experiments with markets, freer speech, and local elections can be bold because they can be reeled in when necessary.[7]

The divide between the princelings and meritocrats does not neatly map across the divisions between left and right. Members of each faction may be attached to different theories of how China should or should not change. Xi Jinping, a princeling, is on the right. Bo Xilai, another princeling, was on the left. It follows, then, that the division can potentially be managed more easily than would be possible if it were both ideological and class based. After all, part of the genius of a permeable elite system is that meritocrats' offspring can become princelings. It just takes a generation for that to occur.

Even while tension persists, however, the strength of a permeable elite system is that the two kinds of elites can coexist for long periods of time. Neither will have the incentive to destroy the system altogether. Even if they hate the princelings, the meritocrats are themselves part of the power structure. They are not on the outside looking in. The princelings will look at the rising meritocrats and fear that their own descendants may not sustain their membership in the elite structure. But the meritocrats want power for their children as well. The princelings recognize that it is therefore unlikely that the meritocrats will eliminate the value of family connections entirely.

In the U.S. system, the two different elites have coexisted since the end of World War II without either one really trying to upend the basic arrangement to which both are committed. For instance, despite their belief in the value of merit as a qualification for success, meritocrats will strive to preserve any hereditary advantages they can for their own children, such as legacy admissions to universities. The flexibility built into a permeable elite system can therefore reduce incentives to revolution in ingenious ways. Compromises may be worked out and new beliefs may be formed in order to justify them.

Rotating Elites: Or, Solving the Transitions Problem

Participants in a democracy usually put a great deal of confidence in the idea that they are expressing their own desires by selecting their own preferred candidates for office. Political scientists who study democracy are much more brutal. Many of them define democracy simply as the rotation of different elites in and out of power through the mechanism of elections. What keeps the system going, according to these political scientists, is not the elections themselves. It is, rather, that when a given elite is in power, it expects to be out of power sometime in the future. Similarly, when an elite is out of power, it expects to get power back. As a result, the elites make a silent, self-interested bargain to respect each other's rights to participate in politics and to hold on to property even when out of power. The key is that elites must rotate. Rolling dice would be as effective a way to make the elites change places as elections. It is just that elections help create the perception of a responsible government.[8]

In China, the princelings and the meritocrats, the key factions within the party, have not developed a reliable way to rotate power between their two factions. If they did, they might be able to transform themselves into normal political parties, split the Communist Party in two, and develop China into a proto-democracy. Such a development might someday occur. But for now, the party would prefer not to take the risk of breaking itself into visible components. Its members would rather retain control as a group and share authority than risk constituting themselves into separate parties that might not be able to trust one another to rotate back into power.

At the same time, however, a version of rotating power does exist in the party's system of transitions. Power is being regularly shifted from one generation to the next. Each cohort of senior Politburo members and Standing Committee members that is selected comes from a particular age cohort of around ten years. No matter how talented you are, you must wait your turn. Princelings receive no advantage when it comes to their age. Neither do meritocrats.

The Confucian tradition of respect for age may have something to do with why this age cohort model of transition works. But Confucianism cannot explain it fully, because Confucian respect for elders traditionally meant that older leaders could cling to power, not be rotated out of office while still relatively healthy. The leaders of Mao's generation, his companions on the Long March, held on into their eighties, as Mao did, and sometimes even their nineties, like Deng Xiaoping. Not so the leaders who rotate out of power today in their late sixties and early seventies to make way for the next generation.

The changing of the guard from one cohort to the next is not exactly the kind of rotation in which groups of elites know that they may personally be out of power, in power, and out of power again. But it offers an alternative that fulfills an analogous goal. As an aspiring leader, the young person knows that he—or least his peers—will get a chance to govern. While in power, leaders know that they will live for many years as ex-officials. They know, too, that their sons and daughters cannot come into power immediately but must bide their time until their own cohort comes of age.

The system creates some distinctive risks of corruption, which I discuss in the next chapter. At its core, however, the Chinese Communist Party has set out to solve the problem of transitions without elections. By publicly rewarding leaders perceived to have done a good job, and excluding those who have not, the party has created the perception of semi-accountability. And by creating a regularized rotation of power, it has eased many of the fears of disorder and disarray that accompany other forms of government such as autocracy.

The success of this model of transitions may be seen in the aftermath of Xi Jinping's two-week disappearance a couple of months before he was slated to become the designated successor as party leader and president. When Xi resurfaced, no official explanation was ever publicly made for where he had been, or why he had disappeared. Rumored explanations did not stop—they just started to seem unimportant.[9] The leader was back. The transition proceeded apace.

The ultimate message, then, of Xi's disappearance was not instability but stability. The fact that the heir apparent could disappear from view without throwing the whole transition process into an uproar suggested just how stable the party apparatus felt to those at the center of it. The party's system for transitions may not yet have reached its full development. But it has shown that it can operate predictably and effectively, even under considerable pressure. This is what transitional legitimacy looks like: when what might otherwise be a potentially devastating crisis is actually a footnote to history.

CHAPTER SIX

LEGITIMACY WITHOUT DEMOCRACY

July 23, 2011, was an ordinary day in Wenzhou, a town in the eastern province of Zhejiang. Just outside town, a brand-new high-speed bullet train was stopped in its tracks on a viaduct over the Ou River. Suddenly, without warning, another new high-speed train plowed into it from behind. The signaling system had failed. Both trains derailed and fell from the viaduct to the river below. Forty people died, and some two hundred more were injured.

As any train buff knows, the new railroad systems of the nineteenth century suffered from collisions, too. China's high-speed rail system is extremely new, the product of an extraordinary push to create the world's largest high-speed rail network in just a few years' time. There is nothing inherently shocking about accidents, even on a modern train line with the latest safety features.

What is significant for our purposes about the Wenzhou derailment is what happened in its wake. At first, information was scarce. In the immediate aftermath of the crash, local government officials and party members circled the wagons in the traditional manner of self-protective bureaucrats everywhere. They engaged in the usual combination of obfuscation, denial, and excuse making. Rather than examining the crash site, they ordered the trains broken with backhoes and buried.

The national rail system, comprising a shocking number of trains on an astonishing number of tracks, is a crucial component of the infrastructure expansion on which the Communist Party has staked its legitimacy. The Beijing-Shanghai high-speed line alone cost hundreds of billions of dollars. The symbolic and practical importance of these trains to China's goal of spreading growth can hardly be overstated. The crash could easily have been seen as a sign that expansion was taking place too fast and without sufficient safeguards. The possibility that corruption was behind the failures of technology could also have been harmful to the regime. Faced with public embarrassment, China's national government initially reacted the way most nondemocratic governments would. It issued only the barest of acknowledgments. The official, party-controlled press said nothing.

Then came the blogs. China's microblogs, called *weibo*, limit the number of characters the user can type at any one time. But because Chinese is written in characters rather than letters, the user can say much more in the space of a few hundred characters than he or she could using the Roman alphabet on Twitter.

Within minutes of the crash, microbloggers were posting comments that, taken collectively, demanded intense public scrutiny. They broke through the cover-up and focused government attention on what had occurred. When a spokesman for the Railway Ministry publicly insisted that the trains had been buried to facilitate rescue efforts ("Whether or not you believe it, I believe it"), the Web exploded, turning his phrase into an absurdist watchword. Eventually China's premier, Wen Jiabao, had to make a public appearance at the crash site to signal that the government was serious about investigating its causes.

Optimistic Western observers saw the microbloggers as harbingers of free speech and democratic responsibility. They drew attention to the technology of microblogging and its censor-defeating speed. The implication of most coverage in the Western media was that public attention to the disaster undercut the legitimacy of the Communist Party. This was consistent with the somewhat self-satisfied Western assumption that only democracy and free speech can produce government legitimacy in the long run.

The Short, Happy Life of a *Weibo*

It is widely assumed that Internet communication, with its immediacy, scope, and variety, is necessarily a threat to nondemocratic forms of government in general and the rule of the Chinese Communist Party in particular. That is not necessarily so. The party might well have seen the microblogging about the train wreck as a gift provided by the technology of the Internet. The public comments enabled the authorities in Beijing to realize immediately that local authorities were engaged in a cover-up. Central authority in a large, dispersed country depends upon effective supervision of local government—which has been a challenge for Chinese governments since the time of the emperors. Local officials cannot always be relied upon to tell the truth and more often shade it to serve their own interests. Getting independent information is therefore a great boon for central control.[1]

The microblogging revealed to officials high up in the party the degree of public concern about what had happened, thus giving the party not only crucial information about a potential blow to its own legitimacy but an opportunity to respond. By taking the crash seriously and eventually sending the premier to address it, the party actually enhanced its own legitimacy. It appeared to be responding to public opinion—because it *was* responding to public opinion. That response took place, it must be noted, despite the fact that neither the premier nor the party was subject to democratic elections. The public, including the microbloggers themselves, saw that the government was prepared to respond to their concerns. And a government that responds to concerns gains legitimacy in the eyes of the people who express those concerns in the first place.

Public posting on the Web in China is closely and constantly monitored by thousands of government censors. The technology of the Internet runs in multiple directions. What people are saying—and what terms they are searching—provides a valuable source of information for the government as to what the general public is thinking. Although immediate public reaction to a particular event cannot be easily controlled, these reactions themselves constitute an instant window into the collective soul of the country.

Even before the Internet, the party had experimented with using the press as a tool for supervising public officials. During the 1990s, newspapers were allowed new latitude to report on social problems and corruption. The press, all of it subject to various forms of party control, was actively encouraged to contribute to improvements in public services by reporting on the failures of local officials. It was not, however, a truly free press. The most important newspapers, for example, typically published two editions—a censored one for the general public and a more open version restricted to high-level party officials. On this model, the press was not an independent fourth estate but a functioning element of the party state.[2]

The Internet offers more direct access to informal supervision and public opinion—at the cost of reduced control. Even with so-called fifty-cent bloggers posting pro-party content for pay, the crowd-sourced comments on microblogs cannot be controlled in the same way as newspaper editors and reporters. A drumbeat of publicly expressed dissatisfaction with how the government is working could certainly prove costly to its legitimacy over time. The party therefore sees robust censorship as a necessary counterweight to the influence of the Internet.

Many topics too numerous to name are prohibited through the

mechanism of the Great Firewall. The religious movement Falun Gong is out of bounds. So is Tibetan independence. The Tiananmen uprising cannot usually be discussed by name. Unsurprisingly, the Chinese government kept close tabs on any Internet discussion of the Arab Spring. Revolution is not a topic that autocratic governments like to indulge.[3]

Maintaining censorship in the era of the Internet poses distinct technical challenges and high costs. (Those who really want to elude the firewall can do it via work-arounds that are developed as fast as they are closed.) But allowing selective free speech can produce tremendous benefits in addition to providing information to the ruling party. It can also help release tension that might otherwise build up in a public frustrated with its inability to speak. Recent research analyzing patterns of social media censorship in China suggests that reactions to news stories, including criticism of the government, are censored less frequently than communication that might lead to collective action or that criticizes the censors themselves.[4]

We know from the examples of totalitarian governments like the Soviet Union that, over time, people unable to speak freely develop secret methods for communicating their values and ideas. The Chinese model of speech regulation is infinitely more sophisticated than that old totalitarian picture. The gamble is broadly that the public will focus on the speaking that it is able to do and pay less attention to the topics that are prohibited.

It remains possible that the Chinese public may become impatient with restrictions limiting its speech to permitted topics—although most evidently accept government censorship of the Internet.[5] Frustration may mount as concerns go unheard. Eventually, some members of the public will want to speak about fundamental rather than simply superficial change. They will, in other words, want to foment revolution.

For the Communist Party to survive, it needs to have a response to those citizens who want to break the system. Having come to power in the form of a revolutionary party, the Chinese communists never forget this possibility. In order to stop another revolution, they need to find ways of producing legitimacy through responsiveness—without losing hold of the reins.

Holding Tight

Maintaining legitimacy in an authoritarian state is extremely difficult. The Chinese Communist Party is engaged in a serious process of trying to solve this challenge and to institutionalize the solutions it is developing. As a result, China's distinct, evolving form of government may—in fact probably will—last much longer than skeptics predict.

I am not talking about permanence; no one should. Democratic government is itself a relatively new phenomenon in historical terms. It has not (yet) lasted anywhere near as long as monarchy. But the Communist Party is developing mechanisms of government that may have the capacity to last many decades into the future—past the point about which we can responsibly speculate. And its chief mechanism is analyzing public opinion, which it monitors as closely as any government on earth.

The party must attend to public opinion so seriously because it knows that it cannot survive as the ruling party without preserving its legitimacy. The trick is to find ways to ascertain public opinion without waiting for serious objections to the system to grow or develop. One method, as we have seen, is surveillance of the Internet. Another classic mechanism is the gathering of human intelligence by a network of party officials and agents. The party has organizational cells within every government-controlled employer and within every neighborhood, block, and even apartment complex. In a sense, all of the 75 million members of the party serve as sources for the handful of party members who do the actual governing.

In addition, like every nondemocratic regime, the Chinese government spies on its own citizens. Contrary to popular belief, this sort of spying does not always or only have to do with identifying ideological deviants. It can also serve the purpose of providing a general picture of public opinion. In World War II, for example, the government of the United Kingdom engaged in systematic surveillance of public attitudes among its own citizens, not primarily to find out what individuals were thinking, but to see what the general trend of public opinion might be. Because it was wartime, facts about public morale were not made public.[6] Indeed, in China as well, the true state of public opinion is a closely guarded secret. From the standpoint of a nondemocratic regime, it ought to be.

Citizen protests are another way for the government to gather information about public opinion. Every year in China there are tens of thousands of protests about everything from corrupt local officials to environmental damage to bad delivery of public services.[7] These unauthorized protests are subject to being shut down as illegal. Local party officials hate them, because they alert central authorities to public dissatisfaction with their performance.[8]

But within some bounds, these protests are tolerated. They can tell local officials what is wrong and encourage them to fix it. They also provide ordinary people in rural areas with a form of leverage over the local officials who govern them. The ruling party fears huge, organized protest marches or demonstrations. The specter of Tiananmen is ever present. But small protests over specific issues need not fundamentally undercut legitimacy. In fact, so long as the public believes that someone is listening, such protests can actually enhance the legitimacy of the overall system.

Corruption and the Rule of Law

Building legitimate, responsive government without holding elections or permitting free speech is a tremendous challenge, one that China has tried to meet in the ways that I have outlined. But China faces a further legitimacy problem bigger than all the others put together, one that threatens the entire edifice of party rule. That problem is corruption. No government can remain legitimate if people think that it is working solely for itself, not for them. Addressing corruption is therefore the most serious challenge faced by the Chinese ruling class. How it manages the challenge may determine the outcome of the cool war itself.

In principle, having a permeable elite should make corruption less desirable for those in positions of power, because they have a chance to pass on some of their power to their princeling children. But in China, tales of the corrupt children of party elites are everywhere. They are even captured in a common, widely known catchphrase: "My father is Li Gang!" This phrase was originally uttered in 2010 by the son of a minor public security chief who was being detained for a drunk-driving incident in which he killed a pedestrian. The outrageousness of his declaration struck a nerve, and the phrase spread rapidly over the Internet. An expression of entitlement and being above the law, it also demonstrates the danger of privilege being passed across generations.

The same concern fueled the demotion of one of President Hu Jintao's closest aides in 2012, after his son crashed his Ferrari Spider in Beijing at four o'clock one morning. The son was killed instantly. Two women with him were seriously injured, and one later died. News reports depicted them as only partially clothed. The story was suppressed for several months but eventually came out. The impression of dissolute princeling privilege was as unmistakable as the $250,000 car.

Corruption costs the Chinese economy billions and perhaps trillions of dollars a year. The government itself estimates that over the last two decades $123 billion of corrupt money was taken out of China by some 18,000 fleeing officials.[9] Ordinary corruption in the course of employment can exist anywhere, but the move from public ownership of assets to partly private ownership presents tremendous opportunities for corrupt officials. In the collapsing Soviet Union, this process produced billionaire oligarchs almost overnight. In China, party officials can take advantage of tens of thousands of new business opportunities and arrogate the profits to themselves and their families.[10]

The scale of corruption in China is great enough to wonder whether it could eventually disrupt the cycle of economic growth. Although in a few countries economic development has proceeded despite corruption—notably Japan, South Korea, and Taiwan—it is generally agreed that corruption is a drag on growth. It certainly distorts the incentives of people making major market decisions— and in China, many business decisions are made by government officials.[11]

More fundamentally, though, corruption undercuts the legitimacy of the system by suggesting that the party is robbing the public to enrich its members. The story of Bo Xilai, the corrupt reformer, raises the possibility that corruption cannot be controlled, even by those who seem logically committed to reining it in. And as everyone intuitively knows, corruption feeds on itself. The more people become corrupt, the harder it is to catch any one of them. As the corruption spreads, the whole practice becomes normalized. Soon, if you aren't corrupt, you are merely naïve.

Taken as a whole, the party wants to fight corruption, because its members do not want to kill the golden goose. Taken individually, however, party members will try to steal as much as they can without getting caught. Fighting corruption requires getting over this collective action problem. As a matter of self-interest, China's elites do not have a collective interest in eliminating corruption altogether. They do have the incentive to keep corruption manageable.

In the West, the dominant solution to corruption has been to establish the rule of law and a system of enforcement. If members of the elite break the law, they will be detected and punished. Fear of punishment is supposed to keep them in line.

The party has taken a slightly different tack. It operates a Central Discipline Inspection Commission, and periodically runs anticorruption campaigns in which thousands of members are investigated and punished. In addition, when party members are shown to be corrupt at the local or national level, the party takes publicly visible steps to purge them. The goal is not to eliminate corruption altogether but to manage it and send the message to the general public that the party cares about stopping it.[12]

A further check on corruption may come from the intense competition among different regional governments to achieve economic success. Winning this competition is the ticket to advancement for regional officials within the party, whose performances are judged by the central party authorities. If corruption within any one region becomes too overwhelming, businesses are likely to locate elsewhere, thereby harming the career of the corrupt officials by lowering economic growth in their region. This competitive system gives individual party officials, not just the party as a whole, an incentive to keep corruption manageable.[13]

Is it enough? That depends on whether the public can ultimately accept the reality of powerful officials becoming rich while still believing that, on the whole, the system is making them better off than they would be if it were to collapse. This is a tenuous balance. Outside experts believe that, in economic terms, the amount of corruption in China is "manageable," and they suggest that levels of corruption have not risen drastically over the last decade.[14] If ordinary Chinese agree, then it is possible that the party can sustain its own legitimacy even in the face of massive corruption.

But party leaders are going to have to get better at managing the public perception of corruption. The Internet could actually help them. If used correctly, public input could help supervise corrupt officials. Anonymous crowd-sourcing can potentially identify bad actors and introduce a bit of transparency to an otherwise opaque system. The so-called human flesh search engine— spontaneous Internet-based activism, where users around the country cooperate to find a particular person who has behaved outrageously—can be a tremendously effective tool for catching wrongdoers. Like other forms of popular justice, the search engine risks targeting the innocent, and the party must be careful to control it. At bottom, though, the party could benefit from popular overenforcement of norms against corruption.

Transitions, the other key component of the new Chinese governance, are also crucial moments to send the message of anticorruption. The public must come to believe that officials who are excessively corrupt are blocked from further advancement. The *nomenklatura* system must be trusted to know not only who is an effective leader but, further, who is so corrupt that his advancement ought to be curtailed.

GOVERNANCE AND CONFLICT

In this part of the book, I have tried to suggest some hypotheses about how China's leadership is trying to develop new, nondemocratic solutions to the problems of governance that democracy also tries to solve. My argument is that, in order to understand how China does and will behave in the cool war, we need to understand the incentives that motivate its leaders—and the internal strategy they seem to be adopting.

China is not on the way to becoming a Western-style democracy. Those who agitate for it, within China and outside, are to be admired for their courage and optimism but not for their sense of political reality. The democratization of the country would put the party's privileges at risk and likely end them. China's leaders are instead seeking to consolidate power for themselves through the gradual expansion of the meritocratic class. So long as the United States continues to challenge the legitimacy of party rule, we can therefore expect continued political conflict between it and China, not only continued geostrategic conflict based on enduring interests.

Yet at the same time, the structure of China's governance experiment also suggests that it may have ways to manage the conflict with the West. The Chinese leadership is highly rational and self-interested. Its interests are tied to continued economic growth, which for now depends on trade ties with the West.[1] Rational actors tend to avoid violence to the extent that they can. They find ways to cooperate. Such cooperation can help the conflict stay cool. It is to the consequences of the cool war—and the possible mechanisms for managing conflict and enabling cooperation—that we now turn.

PART THREE

GLOBAL COMPETITION

CHAPTER SEVEN

THE RACE FOR ALLIES

The ghosts of Pearl Harbor must have stirred in 2012 when Rear Admiral Fumiyuki Kitagawa took his place at the head of a fleet of forty-eight vessels and 25,000 sailors off Hawaii. Second in command of this Pacific armada, Kitagawa was certainly the first Japanese naval officer since World War II to preside over such a formidable array of ships and men. His role was especially striking since Japan's navy, like the rest of its armed forces, is legally restricted to self-defense, a legacy of the pacifist constitution imposed by General Douglas MacArthur.

But the highly visible role played by Kitagawa and the Japanese Maritime Self-Defense Force in the Pacific Rim (RIMPAC) naval exercises—the biggest such exercises in the world—reflected a change in the U.S.-Japan defense alliance. Where once the United States had been convinced that it must handle Pacific security itself, it now sought active partnership with its enemy-turned-ally. Japan, for its part, saw value in strengthening its own military role. The reason for this historic change was the rise of China, the one Pacific power that, Kitagawa smilingly noted in an interview, "was not invited" to join RIMPAC.[1]

Pacific Power

Much of the Cold War was fought through the assiduous efforts of the United States and the Soviet Union to win over frontline states to their respective columns. In pursuit of allies, the two superpowers paid tribute, blackmailed, offered military assistance, and sponsored coups d'état. When they resorted to violence, those flying the planes and driving the tanks were usually the military forces of the proxy states who had become their allies. The Cold War's major strategic developments, from Soviet expansion to containment, détente, and Nixon's opening to China, all clustered around the question of who would be aligned with whom.

The cool war, too, will involve a struggle to gain and keep allies. Like the Cold War and the world wars before it, it will extend wherever there are valuable resources and geographically important avenues for trade and travel. The meaning of alliance, however, will differ from these earlier wars, in which trade between the different camps was severely constricted. In the cool war, the protagonists are each other's largest trading partners. Their efforts to build and maintain networks of allies must therefore be subtler.

In the cool war, each side can try to offer security and economic partnership, but cannot easily demand an exclusive relationship with potential client states of the kind that obtained in the Cold War. Instead the goal will be to deepen connections over time so that the targeted ally comes to see its interests as more closely aligned with one side rather than the other. As in the Cold War, some countries will opt willingly to join the team, some will play the two sides against each other, and others will try to pursue a middle ground of nonalignment. Much more than during the Cold War, key players may try to have it both ways. It will be up to the United States and China to decide how much to tolerate this stance.

Under these conditions, keeping score in the game of alliances will be much harder than it was in the past. But the game itself will remain absolutely central to advances and retreats in the struggle between the United States and China. When wars are fought without shooting, each side's goal is always to weaken the opponent by changing the strategic balance nonviolently. Building new alliances, strengthening those that exist, and weakening the opponent's grip on his allies are the most effective ways to make a difference.

The Pacific region is the first and most obvious place where the game of alliances has begun to be played. The United States established its domination of the region by defeating Japan in World War II. Then, in what is sometimes called a "hub and spokes" arrangement, it made bilateral treaties with Japan, South Korea, Taiwan, and Australia that guaranteed their security without joining them into a single regional alliance on the model of NATO. Although this arrangement was subject to the pressure of a U.S.-China war in Korea and later to a changing U.S. attitude toward Taiwan, it has largely held.

China's economic rise has fundamentally challenged this old order. Over the course of the last decade, China has replaced the United States as the largest trading partner with each of these Pacific countries.[2] The United States remains the key guarantor of security. But increasingly, that security guarantees the capacity of the countries in the region to engage in a free economic relationship with China.

China realizes that its great advantage in building regional alliances comes from strengthening existing economic ties. In November 2012, China joined Japan, South Korea, India, Australia, New Zealand, and the ten members of the Association of Southeast Asian Nations (ASEAN) to announce negotiations for what the group calls a Regional Comprehensive Economic Partnership. Taken as a whole, the proposed free-trade group would include a population of some three billion people with as much as $20 trillion in GDP and approximately 40 percent of the world's trade.

The attempt to build a regional free-trade zone without the

United States represents an alternative to an American-favored proposed Trans-Pacific Partnership that includes the United States but excludes China.[3] Having benefited from U.S. efforts to keep the waterways clear and safe for its export-driven economy, China now does not want to be contained regionally by U.S. proxies. Its long-term goal is to supplant and eventually replace the United States as the most important regional actor. At the same time, it must be careful not to frighten Japan and South Korea so much that they cling to the American embrace. Creating a regional trade alliance that includes traditional U.S. regional allies but not the United States would serve these complicated and slightly contradictory goals. It would provide countries like Japan and South Korea with the incentive to draw closer to China while framing that movement in terms of economic advantage rather than security.

For the United States, the Pacific is ground zero for maintaining its highly valuable traditional alliances with its economic and strategic partners. Its goal is to convince its allies that it is not going away and that they should be very afraid of a dominant China. This would keep those allies close and dissuade them from realigning themselves. At the same time, the United States would like to save money by sharing some of the enormous cost of security. That means sharing some of the responsibility as well. RIMPAC included not only Japan but South Korea, the Philippines, Australia, and New Zealand.[4] The incorporation of a Japanese admiral as the second in command was a signal to Japan and to China alike. The United States was suggesting that it viewed with favor a potential Japanese shift away from pacifism and toward a more active regional security role. At a time when Japan and China were actively jockeying for position around the Diaoyu/Senkaku Islands, this message took on added significance: the United States was willing to empower its allies to keep them in its corner against China.

In response to this American strategy, and spurred by domestic nationalism and by the benefits of moving toward global superpower status, China has not only sought closer trade ties, but has also been increasingly confrontational. It rejects U.S. containment as hostile and unjust. And by threatening confrontation, China signals to its neighbors that it is confident in its rise and cannot be held back. Sensing this confidence, Japan, South Korea, and Australia may decide that it is in their interests to allow China to become a major regional power and not to help the United States contain it. After all, none of these powers wants war. In this way, Chinese aggression could actually encourage greater alliance with its neighbors.

A telling example of a threat generating a possible alliance can be found on the Korean Peninsula, where China's proxy state of North Korea has been openly hostile to South Korea since the 1953 armistice between the two. In late 2010 the North went so far as to shell islands belonging to the South. Yet despite insisting that a firm response is the only way to address North Korean hostility, the South remains open to eventual reunification. How best to engage the North is a recurring political debate in South Korea, but all sides there agree that it should in principle be possible.

China has long used North Korea as a tool in managing its relations with the economically important South. Although no one thinks the unruly North is completely under China's thumb—a point underscored by China's acquiescence to UN sanctions against North Korea in March 2013—the North's aggressive stance makes sense only when seen through the reflected glow of rising Chinese power. A North Korea that fires on its southern neighbor without, apparently, expecting a full-on response suggests confidence in its Chinese backers. South Korea, for its part, relies heavily on U.S. protection but does not want war either with its northern neighbor or with China. In the complicated dance of regional alliances, it tolerates northern hostility in part to maintain good relations with China.

The race for allies may have other unexpected consequences.

One might have thought that the rising Chinese threat would encourage Japan and South Korea into closer mutual relations. Instead, the opposite has been the case. Tensions between the two countries are expressed in a bitter struggle over Dokdo/Takeshima Island and in an ongoing fight over Japan's continuing refusal to pay reparations to Korean "comfort women" who were sexually enslaved by the Japanese military during World War II.

The best explanation for the level of tension is that the unsettling of the regional balance tends to unleash nationalist forces. Both Japan and South Korea were more or less accustomed to their relative positions in the structure of U.S. regional dominance. The prospect that the situation might change means that each side has to reposition itself to a new and advantageous posture. In the past, the United States might have intervened to keep the struggle between its allies under control. Now the United States must be especially careful of appearing to favor either side—at a time when its attention is focused elsewhere. In this case, the cool war is disturbing what were previously understood to be well-balanced regional power arrangements. Today's increasing Japan–South Korea tensions are thus indirect by-products of the rise of China. This result is potentially costly for the United States, which wants to keep Japan and South Korea on the same side, suppressing wherever possible the historical grievances that might plague the relationship. What would otherwise be understandable and minor squabbling now looks like weakness in the U.S.-led alliance.

The Resource Race

Beyond the Pacific, the race for allies can be felt most powerfully in those countries rich in the resources that a growing China needs. From the time of the Cold War, the United States sought a dominant position in the Middle East to ensure a steady supply of inexpensive oil. China has yet to make major inroads in the Arab world, but its energy needs are enormous and growing. It has deepened its relationship with Iran, one of the world's handful of leading oil producers. Here the historical antipathy between Iran and the United States has been valuable to China, which has not had to compete with the United States to acquire this important ally.

Iran needs China's protection against the threat of American or Israeli attack. The protection is political and economic more than military. The United States has tried to isolate Iran economically in order to pressure it to give up on its nuclear program. Iran's economy has been affected, but the country's leadership has not blinked—in no small part because Iran can turn to China for a range of useful trading opportunities. Russia, too, has seen the value of close relations with Iran. As a second-tier power increasingly allied with China, it shares the general goal of weakening U.S. dominance and discouraging American-led regime change, wherever it might occur.

China has also built considerable ties with African states that can promise access to their resources in energy and raw materials.[5] So rapid has been China's expansion into Africa—China became Africa's leading trading partner in 2010—that some have compared it to the European colonial scramble for Africa. The comparison captures something of China's enthusiasm but none of its distinctive strategy. Instead of trying to take over political governance, China typically opts to work with existing governments—whether they are autocratic does not matter—to build infrastructure that is sorely lacking. The Chinese tout their own expertise in rapid development; they bring Chinese labor to do the job; and they promise to deliver the benefits of improved roads, rivers, and revenue streams for government.

They present themselves neither as imperial overlords nor as benign benefactors, but approach African partners in the spirit of businessmen prepared to work with whoever has the capacity to make a deal. Winning over hearts and minds does not seem to be part of the strategy, and the Chinese do not waste time and effort sugarcoating unequal economic deals that result from unequal bargaining positions.[6]

Local African residents will inevitably push back. Chinese abroad seem to be no more culturally sensitive than were their European or American predecessors. But Africans' resistance to Chinese investment will likely look less ideological than did their grandparents' resistance to European colonialism or U.S. imperialism. The difference lies in attitude. China's pragmatic approach to Africa is free of the evangelical spirit and appeals frankly to its interlocutors' naked self-interest—and the Chinese make no bones about the fact that they are pursuing their own self-interest as well. They make no attempt to reform African governance or African ways of life. They may condescend, but they do not lecture. Unlike Western interactions with Africa, the Chinese encounter does not seem plagued by bad conscience.

How much this will ultimately matter to Africans remains to be seen. But a policy of honesty may confer real advantages when dealing with countries and peoples who are accustomed to being met with self-serving lies. China aims to get the benefits of resource colonization without paying the international price of being hated as a colonizer—and it has a reasonable chance of succeeding.

Bad Actors

In addition to honesty, China's pragmatism gives it another important advantage in the race to find allies, one that can be seen pervasively in Iran and in Africa but also throughout the world. Unlike the United States and other Western countries, China typically makes no demands that its allies comply with international norms of human rights or other responsible behavior. In essence, an invitation to allegiance with China functions as a kind of blank check on domestic affairs. As long as your country gives China what it needs, China will not ask what internal processes you used to provide it. What is more, if your practices are challenged in the international sphere, China will offer you cover.

The result of this approach is that many of China's allies are especially bad actors. Iran and North Korea are obvious examples. Another is Sudan, where President Omar al-Bashir has been indicted by the International Criminal Court for crimes of genocide. The list does not stop there. Syria received significant Chinese support in international fora even while President Bashar al-Assad was massacring civilians in response to a popular uprising against him. Myanmar, the former Burma, was a close Chinese ally as long as its military junta maintained its stranglehold on the nation's political life. Its opening toward the United States, driven by the desire to avoid total Chinese hegemony, came in conjunction with the release of political prisoners and promises of future democratization.

China's policy of befriending and protecting bad actors grows naturally out of the party's pragmatism. Not only do the party's leaders not care about the morality of the country's allies, but bad actors are the low-hanging fruit of international alliance. Condemned by the West, states like Sudan and Syria have nowhere else to turn and no other potential champion but China and its weaker ally Russia.

China also has an independent interest in protecting countries that come under significant international condemnation for their treatment of their own citizens. As rulers of an avowed nondemocracy in an increasingly democratized world, China's leaders must advocate for the sovereignty of the state. Any precedent of outside intervention for reasons of human rights violations creates dangers for China.

In the years after the Cold War, thinkers ranging from UN secretary-general Kofi Annan to human rights activists and political philosophers questioned the traditional doctrine of state sovereignty under international law.[7] In different ways, they argued that allowing governments to do whatever they wanted to their own citizens was a moral and practical mistake. These intellectual developments went hand in hand with unchallenged U.S. power. If anyone wanted to override sovereignty to protect citizens against having their rights violated, it was likely to be with the approval of the United States and probably with its active involvement. In the cool war era, this doctrine is highly unattractive to China, a state whose citizens do not enjoy many democratic rights, and which maintains sovereignty over restive populations in Tibet and elsewhere. China's protection of bad actors can therefore also be explained in part by its self-interest in rejecting the idea of humanitarian intervention.

Finally, China's leaders have another incentive to ally themselves with countries that do not respect human rights: self-defense. Liberal democracies can and do band together to enhance their international power and prestige—and their perspective is often both moralistic and missionizing. In doing so they are, implicitly or explicitly, threatening China's political model. As such alliances grow, China's response is to build alliances of its own to counteract those of the liberal democracies. The need for collective international entities can thus arise purely defensively, in a self-fulfilling circle.

A Democratic League?

Running for president in 2008, John McCain openly called for a league of democracies designed to isolate China politically.[8] Since then, the Obama administration has avoided making explicit reference to such an association, for the same reason that it refuses to say that it has a strategy of containment toward China: either position would give ammunition to Chinese hawks who argue for greater defense spending and a more aggressive Chinese strategic posture. Yet the question of a democratic alliance cannot be treated as a taboo in any serious attempt to imagine America's cool war strategy.

Should the United States, the European Union, India, Brazil, and other democracies develop an association that would exclude China and perhaps Russia? To some extent, the military basis for such an alliance is already in place. The United States and the members of the European Union work closely together through NATO. NATO's planned joint military exercises for the summer of 2013, named (a bit quirkily) Steadfast Jazz, will not include Russia. The RIMPAC exercises of summer 2012 excluded China. Economically, the basis lies in substantial U.S.-EU trade. In February 2013, plans commenced for negotiations on a Transatlantic Trade and Investment Partnership that would combine the two partners into a formal free-trade relationship—an epochal development that can be usefully compared to China's attempt to create a regional economic partnership in Asia.

A true league of democracies would extend globally, instead of being restricted to the North Atlantic or the Pacific. To determine if such an alliance would be good for the democracies, we need to consider the issue from the standpoint not only of the United States and Europe, but of the other major global democracies that do not belong to U.S.-dominated regional security alliances—in particular, India. Besides the United States and the European Union, India, by far the world's largest democracy and a close neighbor of China, would be the most important participant in such a league.

During the Cold War, India strove to maintain its independence from either of the two major blocs. Indeed, it led a bloc of its own, the so-called nonaligned movement, that provided shelter and comfort for other states that wanted to stay out of the Cold War. India's reasons for this posture were in part ideological. Its first leaders had socialist economic sympathies and democratic political beliefs, so neither communism nor democratic capitalism quite fit. But the reasons for nonalignment were also instrumental. Master of its own subcontinent, India neither threatened the Eastern and Western blocs nor was especially threatened by them. Border wars with China were worrisome but also brief, as both sides realized quickly that escalation would be disastrous for all.

Today India's global position looks less isolated. Although India still does not threaten any other country (except Pakistan, a special case because of its corresponding hostility toward India), Indian leaders and strategists are increasingly concerned about encirclement by an expansionist China. They worry about the so-called string of pearls, a series of Chinese-built ports in South and Southeast Asian countries, all of which have substantial populations of overseas Chinese. India depends on shipping to get its manufactures abroad, but historically it has never had to maintain a substantial navy. Now it may have no choice but to expand its naval presence in response to the perception that China is encroaching.

India also worries about what China's economic growth might mean for its own recent economic surge. So far the growth in the two countries has been different in kind. China has depended on making things cheaply (and increasingly well), while India has ridden a wave of first-rate human capital to fast, entrepreneurial growth in technology and long-distance services.

These areas of growth are vulnerable to direct Chinese competition. In principle, there is no reason China's top technical universities could not begin to match the high quality of the Indian Institutes of Technology. China's engineers and computer scientists and physicists could rise to the top tier as India's have in recent decades.

Nor is entrepreneurship uniquely Indian—China has a long and recently revived business tradition on which its citizens can draw to start their own companies. India has successfully taken advantage of its immigrant/expatriate community in the United States for business development. There, too, China could do likewise. As for long-distance services, India initially had the advantage of an English-speaking population, but today English speakers can be produced anywhere. China can eventually do what India has done and provide technical support, medical analysis, accounting, and other services remotely.

What is more, China's proven skill in copying designs—for machines, drugs, software, and indeed anything worth making—potentially threatens Indian companies that must protect their inventions or innovations as intellectual property. When it comes to producing ideas, India's advantage could be undercut by China's apparent willingness to borrow, copy, or even steal.

But India cannot easily do what China has done in order to compete reciprocally. India's infrastructure problems make rapid industrialization impractical. The poorest people cannot easily be moved, retrained, or replaced in a democracy the way they can be in China. It is possible therefore for India to see China as a strategic and economic threat, not a passive neighbor pursuing its own independent and noncompetitive path to growth.

India is thus not in the same position as it was during the Cold War. Now nonalignment risks letting China rise to regionally dominant status. India's interest is to balance China in the realm of geopolitics while urging it to respect international law, especially the laws of intellectual property and trade. As a result, India should be increasingly open to joining a democratic league intended to pressure China toward human rights and democracy. It must be careful not to push the Chinese too far. A China that is too isolated might become hostile and bellicose, and India is a weaker enemy than the United States. China could use border troubles with India to feed domestic nationalism. If India were to join the United States in a common league or alliance, it could be depicted within China as a tool of U.S. hegemony.

At the same time, closer ties to the United States would also make India a more formidable opponent to China. We can expect, then, that if the United States were to reach out to India to propose a league of democracies, it might eventually find a receptive partner. The natural ground for the alliance is democracy and human rights—the features that the United States and India share but China lacks.

Democratic Interests

Autocracies and oligarchies tend not to care how anybody else is governed, except insofar as they are frightened by the spread of democracy that might threaten their own legitimacy. Why, by contrast, do democratically oriented countries come to think that democracy should be spread throughout the world?

Ideology plays a major role. Human rights and democracy rely on a set of self-justifications that in turn depend on universal claims. The very term *human rights* suggests that all humans, wherever they are, deserve the basic rights in question. *Democracy,* for its part, suggests rule by the people—conceived as a collection of free individual humans. It is therefore not surprising that citizens who embrace the practices of human rights and democracy begin to accept their justifications and thus come to believe that they are universally applicable. Democracy is, in this sense, an expansionist ideology—a universal theory that tends to promote its own ideals everywhere in the world.

But the universalist appeal of democratic values and human rights is also to the practical advantage of liberal democracies. As new countries embrace human rights and democracy, they orient themselves toward the leaders in these areas—which in practice means wealthy liberal democracies. They then themselves encourage further dissemination of these values. When democracy spreads, these new democracies in turn benefit as earlier adopters of this technology of governance. A positive network externality operates. The more human-rights-respecting democracies there are, the more all of them benefit from their mutual set of ideological commitments.[9]

Countries that respect human rights are also more likely to join cooperative ventures led by other like-minded, rights-respecting democracies. A league of democracies structured by law is therefore plausible in the cool war era. Such an order would serve U.S. interests—because, as a general rule, law serves the interests of the powerful. Legal order protects existing distributions of property and authority. The people who design those institutions are very likely to be the most powerful. They design the institutions in order to make their position legitimate, create stable expectations, and lower the costs of enforcing their will.

Why, then, would weaker, newer democracies ever agree to participate in an international order designed to serve the interests of more powerful, richer democracies? Part of the reason is that people tend to believe that the law is basically just and that following it is the right thing to do. But more important, following the law—and thereby siding with the powers who make it—is generally more advantageous than breaking it. Cooperating with other countries affords extensive benefits in trade and security. Turkey, for example, derived major gains from drawing closer to the European Union during the 1990s and 2000s.

Once joined in a global league of democracies led by the United States, weaker and newer democracies would find themselves allied with one side in the cool war. They could still trade with China, as indeed does the United States. But their political choices in the international sphere would be constrained, much as were those of U.S. and Soviet allies in the Cold War. Wars dictate choices—and growing alliances force smaller players to choose sides.

The upshot is that the United States would have much to gain by spearheading a league of democracies. The ultimate goal would be to contain China, but the basis for achieving that goal would be ideology rather than ordinary self-interest. The United States' advantages in forming alliances derive from its established leading position and from its democratic ideology, which is a real plus in engaging democratic countries. If citizens of many countries can be convinced of the value of democracy for their lives, they will have a long-term reason to prefer U.S. hegemony to a potential Chinese alternative.

For its part, China's advantages in forming alliances presently come from its dynamism, its growth, and above all its undemanding pragmatism, a great help in engaging undemocratic, rights-violating regimes. Faced with a league of democracies, China could respond by emphasizing that its alliance comes with no strings attached. But it would also find itself under pressure to improve its own mechanisms of internal governance and to produce an alternative that might look and sound appealing even to citizens of democracies. If China were to become more democratic, it would render a league of democracies irrelevant.

CHAPTER EIGHT

MANAGING WAR, BUILDING PEACE

In 1795 Immanuel Kant, then acknowledged as the world's greatest living philosopher, published a short pamphlet expressing his vision for creating perpetual peace among nations. His plan was deceptively simple: all states must be republican, they must be arranged into a federation, and people should be allowed to move freely among them. To achieve this plan, armies would have to be abolished, and states would have to give up on borrowing money to build them. States would have to respect each other's internal operations and forswear secret treaties that might lead to war.[1]

The same year Kant's essay appeared, Napoleon Bonaparte rose to fame when troops under his command routed a royalist rebellion in Paris.[2] The next two decades would be spent in wars caused by Napoleon's conquest of Europe and its eventual reversal. A century of relative peace in Europe followed the Napoleonic wars, but World Wars I and II seemed to confirm the impossibility of peaceful international cooperation among competitor states. Kant's liberal internationalism was a dream, his ideas utopian.

The philosopher Thomas Hobbes, by contrast, looked like a dystopic prophet. Hobbes, writing a century and a half before

Kant, had argued that nations were in a permanent state of war with one another—just like individuals in Hobbes's state of nature. For him, the most salient fact about international relations was that no sovereign could tell countries what to do. In the absence of a sovereign, no real society of states, and no international legal order, was possible.[3]

Who was right? Is a stable, peaceful international order possible without an overarching supersovereign, a Leviathan that can govern and make laws for states? Or is the very notion of stable order without a lawgiver absurd?

It is tempting to conclude that Hobbes had the better of it, as most realists believe. They see international stability as a temporary result of either a single overweening power or a fortunate balance of several states. They consider international institutions like the United Nations to be little more than fora for great powers to pursue war ends through the means of politics. And they believe international law to be a contradiction in terms, a semi-organized hypocrisy that nations violate whenever it is convenient.

But in the decades since World War II, the European Union has challenged the realist orthodoxy. Although national identities still exist in Europe, economic, political, and social cooperation has changed people's own conception of their national interests. Western European wars feel historical and anachronistic—even though the last generation to have fought them is only just now passing on. In a deep and apparently fundamental way, the E.U. member states have ceased to think of themselves as geopolitical competitors. Durable, close associations can, it seems, make war obsolete. For the first time in recorded history, we have a concrete example of what Kant sketched.

Internationalists inspired by Kant observe many institutions established by treaty and operating according to law. They see international law being followed as though it were binding, with violators punished and rule breakers sanctioned. In brief, they see cooperation profoundly transforming interests.

The ongoing debate between these two schools is extraordinarily important for understanding the structure of cool war. The unique features of the coming historical period will provide fresh evidence for both sides. But the most important question is whether the participants in the cool war will conceptualize their conflict in terms we can recognize as Kantian or Hobbesian—or both.

The arena where all this will play out most clearly is international institutions and international law. On the one hand, I shall argue, the cool war is going to breathe new life into the United Nations, for a realist reason: the Security Council was designed to manage conditions of great power struggle, and we are returning to a similar situation. On the other hand, some parts of international law are going to start working more and more like the domestic legal systems with which we are familiar—not because there will be a global sovereign but because economic interdependence creates the conditions for mutual legal enforcement.

Back to the Future

The irrelevance of the UN Security Council is coming to an end. The reason is straightforward: we are returning to a global security situation in which the United States will no longer be able to act in what George W. Bush memorably called "a time of our choosing." Increasingly, the United States will have to worry about a Chinese veto in the United Nations and what it would signal about the consequences of acting outside the Security Council framework. The balance of power is changing. The meaning of the veto will change with it.

A recent example of this change could be seen in 2012 when Barack Obama sought to condemn Syrian dictator Bashar al-Assad for his brutal repression of the uprising against him. The previous year Obama had successfully gotten the Security Council to endorse the bombing of Libya, ostensibly to stop Muammar Qadhafi from massacring civilians in his attempt to suppress an insurrection against him. Then, once the air sorties had begun, the United States, alongside the British and French air forces, continued bombing until they drove Qadhafi from power.

When it came to Syria, however, China and Russia used their veto. They believed, with some reason, that they had been tricked into allowing the Libya resolution to legitimize regime change, which they did not support. Although Russia was the closer Syrian ally, China exercised its own veto as well, probably to make the point that it too opposed regime change and objected to more Western-led intervention. Faced with this veto, Obama was encountering a replay of the situation Bill Clinton confronted in 1999 when he could not convince Russia and China to approve a resolution authorizing the bombing of Kosovo to stop a possible genocide there.

Like Clinton, Obama had a precedent of prior Security Council authorization for intervention. He too was facing a new humanitarian emergency in which the Security Council was balking. But unlike Clinton, who bombed Kosovo anyway, Obama seemed to be effectively constrained by the veto. Some senators called on him to arm Syrian rebels regardless of UN authorization, but Obama judged it unreasonable to take overt action over the objections of China and Russia. Naturally, Obama had worries about what would follow regime change in Syria. But as Assad killed civilians in increasingly large numbers, the humanitarian crisis in Syria became many times greater than the one that had arguably been emerging in Libya.

Obama was no dove. He had pursued war in Afghanistan. He had ordered hundreds of drone attacks in Pakistan and Yemen, considered legally dubious by most experts in international law. He had bombed Libya the previous year. The key difference between Libya and Syria was the position of Russia and China, expressed by the Security Council veto. That veto looked utterly different when used by Russia and China in 2012 than it had when exercised by the same countries in 1999. Russia had not become significantly more powerful on the global stage over that period of time. The main reason for the difference was the rise in China's geopolitical power.

The constraints that the rise of China places upon the United States are not exactly the same as the constraints that Soviet power put on it during the Cold War. Without approaching nuclear or conventional parity, China can constrain the United States militarily in areas where the latter would be unwilling to bear the cost of fighting. It can constrain its counterpart economically by issuing a generic threat to reduce (not eliminate) purchases of U.S. bonds, and politically by an unwillingness to acquiesce in U.S. policy objectives on the full panoply of global issues. These options are products of China's vastly enhanced global power, judiciously deployed. As was true of the Soviet Union in the Cold War, China need not promise to go to war when it issues a veto. It need only signal that it might be prepared to retaliate by proxy force, economic means, or politics. As the costs of such a confrontation between superpowers rise, the Security Council will once again become an important forum for managing the possibility of conflict.

Trade and Order: The WTO in Action

The increasing importance of the Security Council during the cool war is a prediction based on the experience of the Cold War. But one international institution has emerged since the Cold War whose importance to the cool war is already a matter of fact. This institution, much more than the United Nations, opens up the possibility of international law that can actually be enforced and that countries will reliably obey.

The World Trade Organization makes news mostly when people protest it, as they did in Seattle in 1999. Seen as an emblem of globalization, the WTO took the brunt of diffuse frustrations having to do with the movement of jobs, the degradation of the environment, and fear of American imperial influence and one-world government. All these concerns did in fact have something to do with the organization's purpose: to make and enforce rules that liberalize trade, the most basic building block of international cooperation.

In essence, the WTO is a forum devoted to facilitating international trade by avoiding trade wars. The member states that sign the WTO treaty promise not to impose barriers to trade on particular goods and services. They promise not to impose tariffs that unfairly discriminate against imported products. Perhaps more important, they also promise to submit themselves to WTO tribunals that will judge trade disputes.

Suppose, for example, the United States thinks that Japan unfairly discriminates against imported American whiskey by imposing higher duties on imported alcohol than on a local, Japanese-made rice whiskey. Japan, in turn, claims that its whiskey is completely different from bourbon, and so the different tax is not discrimination. The United States can go to the WTO and initiate a case against Japan. If the two sides cannot settle the matter on their own, a panel of independent experts will decide the question. The loser may appeal to a permanent appellate body in Geneva made up of independent trade law experts from all over the world. A panel of the appellate body can reverse or modify the decision of the original panel.[4]

Then comes the interesting part. Imagine that the United States wins. If Japan does not back down, the WTO treaty allows the United States to retaliate by imposing a reciprocal tariff on some Japanese import. The punitive tax cannot exceed the total cost of what Japan is doing to the United States. But it does not have to be connected to whiskey. The United States can choose any product it imports from Japan—say, stereos or televisions.

Frequently, a country that wins its case before the WTO tribunal will choose to penalize a particularly powerful domestic industry in its opponent state. The expectation is that the targeted industry will then pressure its own government to end the trade policy that was found discriminatory in the first place. The system is designed to allow the winner to tailor the retaliation however it chooses.

The result is an actual enforcement mechanism. A violator of international trade treaties pays a price—and that price is set by the international panel.[5] At the same time, by regulating the size of punishment, the WTO helps countries avoid escalating a trade war, with its destructive effects. The enforcement mechanism is reminiscent of the schoolyard game where one child is allowed to take a free punch at another without fear of retaliation.

This design provides a powerful example of how international law can actually govern behavior without a true global sovereign that could enforce its rulings through military power. What matters is that the members want to continue to trade freely with each other. That gives them the incentive to respect and obey the judgments of WTO tribunals. If they do not, they will find themselves outside the trade regime that serves their interests generally.[6]

When in the waning days of the Cold War, China began the negotiations that would lead eventually to its joining the WTO, it was still introducing market reforms and did not yet enjoy the explosive growth that would soon follow. During the early years after its official accession in 2001, China, still new to the game of international trade, rarely brought complaints against other countries. Its government chafed when complaints were brought against it. Skepticism toward the WTO reflected China's ambivalence about nondiscriminatory trade policy; it also probably reflected some nervousness about being subjected to the control of an international organization that China was not able to influence.[7]

All that has changed. Now China regularly brings complaints to the WTO, and it just as regularly defends against complaints by other countries. China's skill and sophistication in using the trade regime has been improving. Today students at top Beijing universities participate in model WTO tribunals in the same way that young people all over the world participate in model UN—and they do it in English.[8] These are signs of active buy-in to one of the most effective structures of international law. Like any other powerful participant in a legal system, China aims not only to use the WTO as it exists but also ultimately to shape it according to its interests.[9]

Can the WTO model of enforceable treaties be extended to contexts beyond trade? In the economic realm, it probably can. The WTO itself has expanded its scope considerably over time, including more and more kinds of goods and services. Each round of expansion requires intensive negotiations, and not every expansion has taken place as its advocates would like. But in the most general sense, the direction has tended toward more cooperation, not less.

International treaties governing investment are a major growth area for the enforcement of international agreements in a way that resembles the WTO model. There are some three thousand such treaties in existence.[10] Whereas the WTO has a single overarching structure, the investment treaties are enforced by a decentralized process. But big countries regularly listen to what investment treaty tribunals decide. They take their punishment and reenter the system. NAFTA is the treaty regime best known to Americans. Under it, the United States is sued all the time—and yet the United States has not withdrawn from NAFTA.

The Legal Angle

As the United States and China increasingly cooperate in the economic sphere, and as they increasingly face disputes and tensions around that cooperation, they both will find their common participation in entities like the WTO to be mutually advantageous. Opt-ing out of the treaty and its enforcement mechanism is not really a viable course for countries that participate in global trade. In this context, it would seem that the United States and China must ultimately cooperate.

Cooperation of this type is emphatic proof that international law is really law. It requires formal, binding agreements among states: that is, treaties. Treaties create rules that guide the behavior of the countries that sign them. As such, they are the building blocks of international cooperation—and of international law. When individuals want to make enforceable agreements, they use the legal system created by the state. When states want to ensure that their agreements will be enforced, they need international institutions to do it.[11]

Enforcement institutions like those of the WTO work despite the fact that no supernational sovereign exists. International laws sometimes do get broken—but they also get followed. There are dozens of other treaty organizations, each one created by its own agreement or series of agreements, many interlocking with one another. They may not mete out punishments as effectively as the WTO, but they partake of a similar legal structure. The European Union is the product of international treaties, and it functions as a legal order. It creates laws, and its members follow them. All this international law being followed by states is a crucial component of the cool war world.

What if the WTO model of enforcement through tribunals that allow parties to punish each other were deployed in other contexts beyond the purely economic? Imagine a border dispute between two countries. In principle, a treaty could commit them to submit that dispute to a tribunal. The tribunal would decide for one party. Then the tribunal could set damages. The damages could in turn be valued and paid through trade sanctions, the way they are in the WTO at present.

The basis for this imaginary scheme is the great insight of domestic legal systems: that damages for a wrongful act can be translated into money. Ancient legal systems once dictated an eye for an eye. But very early in human legal history, sophisticated systems began to substitute monetary damages for actual physical retaliation. This model of substitution enabled the legal system to take jurisdiction over a broader and broader range of human interactions.

Many interactions between states could probably be incorporated into international law using the same method of money damages. The difficulty arises when a state willfully tries to violate the rights of another state, say by invading and killing its citizens, and cannot be deterred by the threat of being made to pay damages. What should happen next? Under the WTO model, we would need some analogous forum for retaliation. But today it is difficult to imagine requiring the aggressor state to take a retributive free punch, in the form of allowing some of its soldiers (much less civilians) to be killed.

Reprisals—the technical name for such a punch—were once a familiar feature of state behavior, considered legal or at least common. At the battle of Agincourt, after the French troops killed English retainers and civilian supporters, including boys, Henry V ordered French prisoners killed in retaliation. Today such reciprocal actions are disfavored, even if they sometimes take place.

Under current international law, when a country has been invaded, it is authorized to use violence to defend itself. In this sense, international law already follows something like the WTO model. The difficulty is that defending ourselves against force by using force means that we find ourselves in a war. Each side will continue fighting until some resolution is reached. In this context, we lack the feature of the WTO model that is probably most distinctive: the specification of the amount of retaliation that is allowed by the state that has been hurt by the discriminatory trade practice. In principle, self-defense must be proportional to the threat. In reality, escalation is extremely difficult to avoid. The defending state may plausibly argue that the only way to block the threat is by defeating the enemy in total war.

One alternative is to try to deter war by imposing monetary damages as a punishment after the war is over. This idea, which seems extremely appealing in principle, has been tried in history—with terrible results. In the aftermath of World War I, the victorious Allied forces imposed huge monetary reparations damages on Germany in the Treaty of Versailles. Far from deterring future attacks, the damages became a motivating force for Germany to rearm itself and fight again.

Another great drawback of imposing damages on a government is that a government gets its money from the public, which may or may not be ultimately responsible for the acts its government committed. A similar problem arises when economic sanctions are imposed on an outlaw regime. The sanctions against the government of Saddam Hussein in the years between the first and second Gulf wars had serious and terrible consequences for ordinary Iraqis, who were not themselves personally responsible for what Saddam had done.

But it is worth noticing that the WTO model also does not impose penalties directly on the entity that is responsible for the unfair trade practice. Indeed, sanctions under the WTO are frequently aimed at private industries. Those industries employ ordinary people, who are not responsible for the policies their governments have enacted. Despite this common feature with other international sanctions, however, the WTO scheme is rarely criticized for this anomaly. To the contrary, the system is praised for allowing the injured country to choose what area of economic interest to target for its sanctioned retaliation. It follows that the apparent injustice of sanctioning citizens for the acts of their government might be overcome. Perhaps, then, monetary damages could be reintroduced as an antiwar deterrent, provided they were not excessive.

If such problems were solved, a WTO-like tribunal could become an effective mechanism for managing violent international conflict. It would be too optimistic to predict that such solutions will emerge during the cool war. But the cool war does create the conditions of interdependence and law following where such thinking outside the box is possible—and it creates the incentives to try it out.

Pursue Peace and Prepare for War

The optimistic neo-Kantian argument is bolstered by international institutions like the World Trade Organization that lay down legal obligations for their member states to follow. Frequently—indeed, most of the time—nations seem to obey these laws. If the world is fundamentally a place of unregulated competition among states, why do such institutions speak in terms of cooperation, and why does cooperation exist so broadly?

The realist response is that states cooperate situationally in order to manage the ultimate competition among them. Competition can be deeply destructive if it goes too far. If states miscalculate, their arms races may become all-out wars. Their trade disputes may become punishing trade wars. Cooperation therefore is what states do so that competition does not swallow them up. International law may soften the harsh realities of competition, but it cannot fundamentally alter them. The moment a state's desires change, and the benefits of breaking free outweigh the costs of staying within the treaty, the treaty regime will be violated.

The Cold War provided substantial evidence to support the realist picture of international cooperation. The United States and the Soviet Union both used the United Nations to try to manage the risks of global nuclear conflagration. They met in the United Nations to discuss their problems; but their weapons were pointed directly at one another the entire time.

Faced with the difficulty—or perhaps the impossibility—of knowing whether true cooperation is possible or competition is inevitable, both the United States and China are propelled toward a dual strategy. To put it simply, both sides in the cool war will behave as though they truly do not know whether their cooperation will be successful. Both sides will act like European cooperators, sincerely trying to change and make cooperation into the fundamental feature of their bilateral relationship. At the same time, both sides will also have no choice but to prepare for war.

States are not abstractions. They are products of beliefs and actions by real people, with real interests. China's leaders, now and in the foreseeable future, will always have the overarching incentive to keep themselves in power. Above all, China's leaders will not have the incentive to make China anything less than a fully sovereign state. They are profoundly unlikely to view the United States as a potential political partner in the way European states see one another.

Both sides will no doubt continue to pursue strategies of cooperation and see their states as well served by a binding web of international legal agreements. But it follows that, in pursuing cooperation, the United States and China will eventually hit its limits, due to the particular incentives and ideas of China's leadership. Those limits will in turn drive both sides to maintain the structures and ideas associated with realist geopolitical confrontation—of containment on one side and military pressure on the other.

The persistence of realism need not, however, mean that the relationship between the United States and China must be structured by inevitable conflict. Just as all sides must recognize the possibility, indeed the probability, of eventual conflict, all sides must also rationally acknowledge the likelihood of extensive and deepening cooperation—to mutual benefit. The Chinese elite cannot at present survive direct confrontation, because a rapid decline in economic growth would destroy its economic interests and popular legitimacy. For now, therefore, the Chinese leadership must have cooperation to survive. This need for cooperation will continue into the foreseeable future. Given this incentive, cooperation has the capacity to change incentives on both sides very drastically.

In a cool war situation, international institutions can function both to manage the conflict of opponents who do not share a legal framework and also to provide a venue for common cooperation under law. The Security Council, designed to manage conflict between Cold War opponents who were in Hobbesian anarchy with each other, will play a version of that same role for the United States and China. Simultaneously, international trade law will function as a real, enforceable neo-Kantian legal order because of economic interdependence. That interdependence could potentially be leveraged to subject some aspects of war and peace to similar law-like regimes, even without a supersovereign capable of enforcing its own judgments. That these developments will occur at the same time may seem paradoxical—but that is precisely the paradox of cool war.

CHAPTER NINE

CORPORATE COOL WAR

When Google was founded in 1998, the two Stanford graduate students behind it—one of them an immigrant from the former Soviet Union—made much of their rallying cry: "Don't be evil." Six years later the company had to decide whether to launch its Web search operations in China. The condition for one of the world's fastest-growing companies to enter one of the world's fastest-growing markets was that Google accept Chinese government restrictions on content. This was the first major test of Google's unofficial corporate motto.

As it turned out, the meaning of *evil* offered plenty of room for maneuver. Telling itself and its shareholders that operating in China would in the long run enable information to become free there (or at least freer), Google accepted China's conditions.

The experiment failed. Google China was not able to achieve a significant market share on the mainland. Then its servers were subjected to cyber attacks that, according to leaked State Department cables, were directed by the Chinese government itself and possibly even by a member of the Politburo Standing Committee. Citing concerns for free speech—concerns it had been grudgingly prepared to suppress in pursuit of corporate profit—Google abandoned the Chinese market.[1]

Before giving up entirely, however, Google used a highly creative strategy to try to pressure China into allowing it a fair shot at achieving market share. Through nongovernmental organizations that it funded, Google approached the office of the U.S. trade representative to complain that the Chinese government was discriminating against it in the delivery of online services. The content restrictions, Google suggested, amounted to unfair treatment of Google relative to Chinese Web search companies like the market-leading Baidu. This discrimination, Google claimed, violated trade agreements between China and the rest of the world. Google wanted the U.S. government to haul China before a WTO panel.[2]

There is nothing uncommon about a company that is having trouble in a foreign market asking its government to consider allegations of trade discrimination. What made the case unusual was the content of Google's claim. Google was saying that China's restrictions on free speech discriminated against Google. Its theory was that online services needed to be freely available to be nondiscriminatory. In essence, Google was trying to get a human rights claim before the WTO.

Needless to say, Google was not acting out of a principled commitment to human rights. A corporation is organized for profit, not principle—and Google had already shown its willingness to compromise its nominal principles to enter the Chinese market. Instead, Google was trying to use human rights and international law to embarrass the Chinese government and improve its negotiating position. It was using emerging cool war realities to put pressure on China and the United States alike. To do so, it had to appeal to U.S. nationalism and national interest to convince the U.S. government to advocate on its behalf in the forum of international law and in the language of human rights. Having engaged in cooperative trade with China, Google was now trying to generate competition between China and the United States.

Doing Business the Cool War Way

Google's experience in China—and its brief foray into human rights advocacy—holds important lessons for understanding how corporations will negotiate the complicated global spaces of the cool war and what corporate participation in the cool war will mean for the other players.

The first lesson is that our standard picture of a company's identity as a national or transnational entity is going to change. Google, a global firm headquartered in the United States, is a for-profit corporation whose primary duties run to its shareholders. But Google's competitors for search services in the Chinese market were Chinese corporations—notably Baidu—that see their identity and their purposes differently. Baidu grew to control 80 percent of the market after Google's withdrawal. Although Baidu is a for-profit company that sells shares on NASDAQ, not a state-owned enterprise, Baidu's founder and CEO, Robin Li, makes great efforts not to anger the party. Li realizes that long-term profitability in the Chinese market depends on fulfilling the party's demands and needs. Party officials are not shy about expressing their preferences, directly or through state media outlets. Li understands the need for rapid response.[3]

Something of the kind was on show when, in the summer of 2011, the Beijing party chief marched into the offices of Sina Weibo, the market-leading microblogging service, and told its executives he expected that the company would "absolutely put an end to fake and misleading information" on its site.[4] This was no easy challenge for a site where users post content in real time. Nonetheless, by summer 2012, Sina Weibo had invented and introduced its own self-censorship for its users. (Customers start with 100 points and lose points for telling untruths, criticizing the government, or other inappropriate Web behavior. If they run out of points, their accounts can be suspended.) Sina Weibo's marketing department can hardly have believed that introducing the system would increase usership or loyalty to the product. The point, rather, was for Sina Weibo to demonstrate loyalty to the party, even at the cost of displeasing customers.

Even in the West, a fast-growing firm must keep an eye on the government. Just ask Microsoft, which faced a major antitrust suit in the late 1990s that could have seriously harmed its business model. Google has lawyers and Washington lobbyists and all the other apparatus of a major corporation that must manage what are euphemistically called "government relations." Competing firms have the same array of weapons. All understand that using lawsuits and government regulation as a tool to attack one's competitors is within the rules of the game. But none of Google's domestic competitors was actually devoted to serving the interests of the U.S. government. Like Google, they were focused on their shareholders.

It is one thing to compete with another private firm. It is quite another to compete with a firm that is deeply influenced by the forces that run the country where the market is located. Google swamped its search competitors in the United States and Europe by creating a better product, marketing it, then figuring out how to make a profit by selling advertising. The same approach was no guarantee of success when its competitor was in bed with the Chinese Communist Party.

De facto party oversight is a mixed blessing for companies like Baidu, as it is for all other major Chinese firms that depend on the party to flourish. The party's interests can stand in the way of the most profitable strategic choices, and the firm's executives must consider closely the political meaning of all crucial business decisions. But there are also huge benefits for a company so closely tied to the party: when push comes to shove, the party may be prepared to protect it from competition. The cyber attacks on Google demonstrate that the party did not want Google to dominate the Chinese domestic search market. The limitations on Google's ability to operate were themselves constraints on Google's business model, which is aimed at maximizing the user's access to information. Baidu was the fortunate beneficiary of that preference. More precisely, Baidu was functioning as a tool of the party, which is one of the few entities on earth significantly more powerful than Google.

Google may not have fully anticipated this possibility when it entered the Chinese market. Faced with the reality that the party strongly favored its chief competitor, Google found itself trying to align its interests with one of the handful of entities on earth more powerful even than the Chinese Communist Party. That was the government of the United States, to which Google turned in the hopes of finding a champion.

In order to get the U.S. government's help, Google judged that it should try to advance a legal claim. Since it could hardly sue the Chinese government in Chinese courts, Google had to appeal to international law. In the realm of trade law, as in most other areas of international law, a corporation cannot itself bring a claim. Only a government may go to the WTO on behalf of a company and allege a breach of international law.

The upshot was that Google had to behave less like a transnational corporation serving the interests of its shareholders than like an American firm seeking to convince "its" government to help it out. As part of this effort, Google aligned itself with the universal human rights value of free speech. This was a canny and not coincidental strategy. Google hoped that the U.S. government would, for its own reasons, welcome the opportunity to criticize China for a human rights violation.

The consequence is that if transnational corporations wish to compete with Chinese firms controlled by the party, they ultimately need their own governments to help them level the playing field.

Western-based, for-profit corporations will still define themselves in terms of their shareholders' interests. They will still do business with China, as Google still does in areas other than search technology. But serving their shareholders will now require them to identify themselves to a greater degree than before with the governments of the countries where they are based.

In recent decades there has been much discussion of transnational corporations as true freelancers, moving capital easily from place to place and acting without much concern for their states of incorporation. Increasingly, those companies that must compete with Chinese opposite numbers will have to consider how they can align their interests with those of their home countries. Cool war will not eliminate the mobility of transnational corporations, but it will make them look for governmental allies, and remind us that states, not corporations, remain the primary locus of ultimate global power.

New Risks

A second, related lesson of Google's China endeavor is that cool war conditions introduce new types of risk to business ventures. When Google chose to expand into China, it naturally weighed the ordinary business risk that the venture would go badly and fail to attract a sufficient number of users. But there were other risks as well, distinctive to the new situation.

One was that the Chinese government would engage in cyber attacks on Google's operations, either to steal its intellectual property or to otherwise affect its business operations. Industrial espionage is nothing new. A French Jesuit stole the secret of China's porcelain manufacture in the seventeenth century.[5] Many advances of the Industrial Revolution were stolen from England and brought to Europe and the United States. Industrial sabotage also has a long history.

But cyber attacks are a particularly effective, deniable, and transnational medium for espionage and sabotage. China has broken new ground by introducing a significant government role in shaping these familiar tools of international economic competition. As a result, cyber attacks are not simply a facet of international competition. They are also a component of war.

Increasingly, concerns about cyber attacks and the theft of intellectual property will no longer be limited to firms that, like Google, are entering the Chinese market for the first time. Geographical proximity is not an important constraint in the cyber world. Any firm that finds itself on the opposite side of a serious Chinese competitor can now expect to be subject to governmentally sanctioned warfare.

Another new kind of risk that Google faced was that it might lose some of its cachet as a do-gooding brand by agreeing to work with Chinese censors. This might seem like a relatively small danger, one unique to a firm founded by idealists (or at least people who knew how to sound like idealists). In fact, though, the risk of looking bad by virtue of collaborating with Chinese actors is not small. And it turns out that, under cool war conditions, many more firms than in the past have a significant stake in looking like they are good actors.

Any business endeavor that requires a foreign firm to work within China exposes it to the criticism that it is dealing with an autocratic regime. Google faced the ignominy of working with censors. Manufacturing firms have to grapple with the charge that Chinese workers are underpaid, badly treated, and denied access to unions—or even that Chinese factories use child and slave labor. Apple, for example, has struggled with allegations that iPhone parts made in China are the products of substandard labor conditions.

Once such an allegation has been made, it can affect marketing. The costs become especially serious if and when the firm finds that it wants to position itself as a representative of Western values. Apple does not market itself as an exponent of human rights, but it does market its products as the embodiment of individualized autonomy. Indeed, an essential part of what makes the brand unique is that its devices are designed to become an extension of the user's self. The ideal of the self-possessed, creative Apple user personalizing her device to match her lifestyle becomes harder to sell when we imagine Chinese children coerced into working on its parts. In the realm of marketing, facts matter less than perceptions, and the idealized perception of a product is an asset that is easily squandered.

Too Big to Succeed

The last and most significant type of new risk that Google faced in China was that it would not be allowed to succeed in the Chinese market simply because of the nature of its product. Google emerged as a household name, its product entering the language as a verb, because its search engine facilitates the act of sorting through vast amounts of information. Information may or may not want to be free, but it is certainly not useful unless it can be organized. The organization of information in turn is most valuable if the user can be relatively confident that it has been drawn from an unlimited pool. It follows that the phenomenon of Internet search is at its core about getting specific knowledge from the broadest possible universe of sources.

From the perspective of the party, Google's virtues were disadvantages. To maintain its position, the party must control the flow of information to some degree. That means that it must restrict search. The user wants to know as much as possible as fast as possible about the topic of her query. The party wants to restrict quantity, speed, and topic—all the essential elements of search. For the party, it would have been extremely risky to allow the rise to dominance of a player with the profit-driven incentive to increase the flow of information.

Had Google come to dominate the Chinese market in the way that it dominates the search engine market in the West, it would have become a significant player in the construction of informational life in China, much as it is in the West. Even if Google China had continued to operate under censorship, Google would have had a permanent, long-term incentive to reduce that censorship and minimize the party's control. Google's motive to fight censorship did not lie in the moral values of its executives. It lay in the nature of Google's product.

The risk that a successful foreign competitor might not be allowed to succeed in China extends beyond the information-related search business. Many other industries play important roles in shaping social and political life. Steel manufacturing is a sine qua non of industrial development. Big-box stores tend to drive small shops out of business, affecting patterns of entrepreneurship, land use, and urban planning. Sellers of branded consumer goods market a lifestyle that may or may not be consistent with the party's plans for the development of a domestic consumer economy. Large-scale employers set wages and conditions, thus affecting the expectations of their competitors' employees. In all these cases, foreign firms engaging with China must confront the risk that, for essentially political reasons, they will not be allowed to defeat their Chinese competitors.

Just as important, when Chinese firms are party controlled, they generate power and revenue for party members. Senior party officials and their family members and close associates are likely to have investment stakes in important Chinese firms. The party itself will control the boards of directors of state-owned enterprises and will likely maintain this control even if those firms are gradually privatized. Party members will therefore almost always have incentives to limit the success of foreign competitors—no matter how innocuous the effects of the business's profile. In cool war China, economic competition cannot be separated from political power.

Tools of Trade

To mitigate the risks of doing business in a cool war environment, Google sought to align itself with human rights and to lodge an international law claim against the Chinese government. As it happens, the U.S. government publicized the issue by commencing its own investigation and asking China to account for the treatment of Google. It has not, however, formally filed a WTO claim against China in the Google matter.

If the United States did file a trade claim against China, could it work? Did China's treatment of Google actively violate any WTO provisions? And if it did, might other businesses be able to swath themselves in the cloak of human rights and bring similar claims?

To win before a WTO panel, the country bringing the claim must show that the other country discriminated against foreign firms in favor of domestic ones. Most trade experts who have looked at the Google claim have concluded that it would be difficult for the United States to show that China had in fact discriminated against Google relative to Baidu or other Chinese-based search firms. Google sought to argue that limits on the free flow of information themselves violated the principles of international trade law. But this is not precisely the same thing as discrimination. After all, Baidu was subject to the same content restrictions as Google. Limitations on free speech applied to both. If the limitations are truly equal, it is difficult to see where the trade violation lies.

The counterargument is that, in practice, China's goal was to ensure that local companies, susceptible to party control, maintained a dominant share of the search market. The same is true with respect to blogging and social networking. This goal certainly violates the rules of international trade. It is based fundamentally on discrimination in favor of local firms that are likely to be compliant when dealing with government censorship. By limiting Google, China achieved this goal.

The challenge would be to demonstrate this pattern in a way that would be clear to an impartial, legal decision maker like a WTO tribunal. The formal neutrality of China's censorship rules—that is, the fact that they apply to Chinese and foreign firms alike—functions as a kind of shield for China. If the United States were to pursue the claim on Google's behalf, it would have to focus on the fact that Chinese firms are more likely to be influenced by the party itself. This reality shows why censorship rules can place foreign firms at a special disadvantage.

The harassment of Google by cyber attack is a highly convincing piece of evidence to prove discriminatory treatment. Google itself seems to have known that the Chinese government was behind the attacks on its servers. The intelligence services of the U.S. government must have played a role in investigating the attacks and trying to trace them. If the evidence tracing the attacks could be revealed without sacrificing national security, then the United States could introduce and suggest the existence of the pattern.

In the foreseeable future, then, it may be possible for the United States to convince a WTO panel that a firm like Google has been subject to systematic discrimination in order to reduce or eliminate its market share within China. Firms facing such discrimination should increasingly be able to convince their home governments to pursue their claims. In essence, the WTO could become a front for a counteroffensive against the party's preference for firms that it controls.

The Party in Corporate Form

The cool war will not only affect international firms competing with Chinese businesses. It will also affect Chinese firms operating abroad. Indeed, if someone were to ask when the first shots of the corporate cool war were fired, the answer might well be June 23, 2005. That was the day the state-owned China Natural Offshore Oil Company (CNOOC) launched its $18.5 billion bid to buy the huge U.S.-based oil company Unocal.

For China, the acquisition would have helped assure an adequate and reliable supply of oil at a reasonable price—a crucial necessity for a growing economy.[6] But even in 2005, well before the economic downturn that shook the United States, and before China's rise had become an important topic in domestic public debate, U.S. politicians were fearful of a foreign firm owning a huge resource-producing American one. The price of oil, which was rising at the time because of the Iraq War and China's growing demand, did not help matters. By early August, rebuffed by Congress, CNOOC withdrew its bid.[7]

For CNOOC in particular and expansion-oriented Chinese firms in general, the experience left deep scars. The bid had been too much, too fast. CNOOC had been perceived as an economic invader: the Chinese government in corporate form. At a sensitive moment in the global energy market, trying to buy an asset as important as Unocal had been clumsy. CNOOC had managed, altogether unintentionally, to create significant nationalist anti-Chinese sentiment in the United States. Instead of improving China's global strategic situation, the bid had set it back.

In the wake of the CNOOC-Unocal controversy, it would be easy to assume that during the cool war, national corporations and strategic industries will not be able to make major acquisitions in the heart of their opponents' territory. Indeed, this would seem to be consistent with the lessons of the Google controversy, in which a U.S. company was ultimately unable to make inroads into the Chinese market in the strategically important area of search.

Yet in the summer of 2012, seven years after its failed bid for Unocal, CNOOC tried again. The new target for acquisition was the Canadian energy firm Nexen. CNOOC's $18 billion-plus offer had to be approved by the Canadian government and at least in part by the United States. This time there were strong reasons to believe the carefully crafted deal would go through—reasons grounded in the logic of the cool war.

To begin with, CNOOC did not go after a Canadian firm whose primary assets are located in Canada. Nexen gets just 30 percent of its oil revenues from Canadian sources, the rest coming from offshore holdings in the North Sea, Nigeria, and the Gulf of Mexico. Had CNOOC been trying to buy a company whose core business was in Canadian territory, it might have looked like a would-be imperial power getting a foothold in North America. By acquiring assets scattered around the world (albeit controlled by a single firm), CNOOC looked more like yet another global player in an industry that is itself global.

Above all, CNOOC wisely sought its North American takeover target in Canada, rather than the United States, where anti-Chinese nationalist sentiment was likely to be higher. From Canada's perspective, enhanced economic ties to China are almost wholly positive. For reasons of geography and history, Canada will always be closely linked to the United States. Its security is assured so long as the United States cares about its own security. It therefore has every incentive to free ride on that implicit security guarantee while taking advantage of Chinese direct investment to improve its trade balance. In the Cold War context, Canada would have to have been extremely careful about crossing the aisle to do a deal with the Soviet Union. In the cool war, security alliances with one side can be reconciled with economic relationships to the other: indeed, that is the central characteristic of cool war.

CNOOC still needed regulatory approval from the United States and Britain to close the Nexen deal, since Nexen has wells in American and British territorial waters. These were not sought until Canadian approval was officially granted in December 2012. From that point forward, however, the United States and Britain both had interests in respecting the Canadian decision. For either U.S. or U.K. politicians to spoil a primarily Canadian deal would be costly for their own relations with Canada. CNOOC had, in other words, managed to build a strategic alliance with Canada for the purpose of getting a deal approved. It was securing a political beachhead, not by force but by negotiating skill.

The CNOOC-Nexen deal underscores a different set of lessons for international business than does the Google-China controversy. First, even a state-owned Chinese company can make major acquisitions abroad if it picks its targets carefully. It might have been reasonable to expect that, in the medium term, Chinese firms would have to reduce their degrees of state control in order to be treated as legitimate foreign investors. The Nexen acquisition shows that this is false. If CNOOC can make sensitive acquisitions abroad and receive approval from foreign governments, firms that are not wholly state owned but that are subject to party control should be at least as capable of buying foreign targets.

Second, exquisite political sensitivity must be part of target selection. If CNOOC could not acquire Unocal in 2005, when the cool war had not yet been acknowledged, it almost certainly could not have acquired a major U.S. energy company in 2012. But by choosing a Canadian firm—and more than that, a Canadian firm whose assets were primarily offshore—CNOOC had a chance of grabbing the prize. Big acquisitions are, in the cool war context, moves in a grand strategic game. They must be taken extremely carefully and with considerable forethought given to how they will be received in the targets' home countries.

Third, and most important, economic interests may be used as leverage to shape political outcomes. Canada's need for foreign direct investment is certainly what motivated its government to permit the acquisition. But CNOOC's real brilliance lay in structuring the process of regulatory approval so that Canada would become its ally in seeking second-stage approvals from the United States and Britain. In the broadest sense, Canada's geostrategic interests lie much closer to those of the Americans and the British than to the Chinese. Notwithstanding this alignment, it was still in Canada's interests to have a deal approved by its allies once it had judged it to be in its own domestic interests. Over the long term, the closer economic relationship between China and Canada that will emerge will subtly draw their political interests closer together.

Cool War Corporations

Multinational corporations depend on stable legal relations between countries and so are sometimes seen as harbingers of a postsovereign world where power is widely dispersed and capital can outweigh force as the leading driver of human affairs. The examples of Google and CNOOC help show that in a cool war world, the dominance of the multinational corporation will not be so absolute. On the one hand, Google, despite its tremendous size and skill, was unable to penetrate the Chinese market, mostly because it was too big to succeed without threatening the party. On the other hand, CNOOC, despite being an arm of the Chinese government, was ultimately able to make a North American acquisition—largely because the government found a way to make it in Canadian interests.

The point is that in the cool war, corporations must contend with powerful state actors and do so in new ways. They must be able to identify with their home countries and also disidentify from them when needed. Above all, major multinational corporations will need to be constantly aware of and vigilant about the broader economic and political consequences of their own actions and roles. As the distinction between global economics and geopolitics breaks down, the distinction between business and politics is breaking down with it.

CHAPTER TEN

THE FUTURE OF HUMAN RIGHTS

In May 2012, Secretary of State Hillary Clinton and Secretary of Treasury Timothy Geithner were poised to make a rare double visit to China for a high-level strategic and economic dialogue. The presence of both of these key cabinet officials at a delicate moment in the relationship between the two countries marked the importance of the issues. For once, economic interdependence and geopolitics were on the agenda at the same moment.

But on April 22, in the tiny village of Dongshigu in the eastern Shandong province, something happened that would eclipse the visit. Chen Guangcheng, a blind dissident lawyer-activist, managed to scale a high wall to escape the building where he had been under house arrest for two years. Chen broke his foot in the process, yet over the next several days, with the help of other activists, he managed to make his way four hundred miles to Beijing, where he was taken into the U.S. embassy. On April 27, when he was inside the embassy, a YouTube video was posted in which Chen informed Premier Wen Jiabao that he had escaped and demanding punishment for the local officials who had detained him.

In the days that followed, Chen's future became an international incident of the highest order. Chen first insisted he did not want to leave China. Then, after he was transferred to a Chinese hospital to have his foot treated, he changed his mind. In an emblematic piece of cool war theater, Chen, from his hospital bed, used a borrowed mobile phone to address an open hearing of the U.S. Congress in Washington. He told the congressmen—and the world—that he was worried for his family's safety and wanted to come to the United States.

Chen's predicament, featured for days on the front pages of the U.S. press, drew Western eyes away from the secretarial visit. Finally, after days of intense negotiations between ranking U.S. diplomats and their Chinese counterparts, Chen obtained permission to travel to the United States as a special student, a "solution" that spared China the embarrassment of having Chen granted asylum status. The pressing questions of politics and economics that were supposed to be the subject of the visit were ignored, replaced by the subject of human rights.

The Chen Guangcheng episode hints at the hugely complicated and hugely important way that human rights will figure in the cool war. The United States showed a willingness to put human rights issues front and center even when other issues were supposed to be on the table. The upstaging of a major diplomatic encounter by a focus on China's human rights violations may conceivably have been planned by someone within the U.S. government, since the whole story of Chen's escape seems highly improbable without help. Even if the timing of Chen's escape was accidental, the U.S. embassy still had to decide to take Chen in, creating an inevitable crisis. Either way, the United States knowingly put human rights first in a highly public forum.

From the Chinese standpoint, the whole episode must have been frustrating and embarrassing. Enormous diplomatic resources went into discussing the fate of one previously little-known human rights activist. Instead of being treated respectfully as a rising global power, China was being scolded as a rights violator. The United States seemed to be using human rights to weaken China and give itself an edge in discussions between them.

The emerging historical moment is creating a new context for the rhetoric and practice of human rights. For the first time since the fall of the Soviet Union, the United States now has a major incentive to promote the international human rights agenda. So long as China continues to violate human rights, there may be no better ideological tool for the United States to gain advantage under cool war circumstances.

To understand the trajectory of how human rights will matter and be used in the coming era—and to predict how China will respond—we need to turn back to the origins of our ideas and practices of human rights. The combination of sincere belief and cynical manipulation in the human rights realm goes back to the end of World War II and the Cold War, and it demonstrates how power politics will necessarily shape the development of human rights in the future.

Cold Rights

Since the Nuremburg tribunals, it has been accepted in principle that the world should try to bring to justice the worst violators of international humanitarian law, which applies in wartime.[1] The Nazi trials were not all they are sometimes remembered to be, and many contemporary observers believed they were little more than victors' justice.[2] Nevertheless, they did create an important new precedent. For the first time, members of a government were held criminally responsible by an international body for harms to individuals that they committed while in power. In this sense, at least, universal human rights were demonstrated, declared, and acted upon.

Then, from a practical standpoint, nothing much happened.

Early in the Cold War, the United Nations adopted the Universal Declaration of Human Rights. That document, however, was not law. It was not even international law. It was called a declaration because it was, in legal terms, a hopeful, aspirational statement of ideals, but it had no enforcement mechanism and no legal commitment by the signatories to follow it.

For most of the next twenty-five years, the topic of human rights rarely figured in American political rhetoric at the international level. It is not hard to see why. Until 1954 the United States had a formal, legal system of government-mandated segregation in place in many of its states. Until 1964 no federal law expressly prohibited racial discrimination by businesses. The next decade was spent in the painful process of trying to negotiate racial integration, not only in the American South, but in Northern states where segregation operated on a de facto basis even though it had not been enshrined in law. During these years, the United States had a great interest in avoiding public discussions of human rights. The Soviet Union, for its part, was able to point to race discrimination as evidence of U.S. hypocrisy.

In the middle of the 1970s, things began to change.[3] Having greatly reduced its vulnerability to the charge of institutional racism, the United States could use the ideology of human rights to attack the Soviet Union. The presidential administration of Jimmy Carter began to institutionalize human rights criticism. Congress mandated annual country reports to monitor human rights violations around the world, including among U.S. allies. This was recognized at the time as something new, even humorous. Cartoonist and political commentator Garry Trudeau created a new *Doonesbury* character—a pleasant, ineffectual human rights officer in the Carter State Department—and had him present various absurd awards for human rights "compliance."[4] The effect of these cartoons was not primarily to accuse the U.S. government of hypocrisy, but to note rather sweetly the irony that this Cold War power was beginning to speak the language of rights instead of power.

At the same time, Eastern European dissidents, at great personal risk, signed documents like Charter 77 that condemned the Soviet system for violating human rights, to which it had made a symbolic commitment in the 1975 Helsinki Accords. This was a new strategy, a product of the Brezhnev era. The dissidents were making a play for Western attention and the support of Western governments—and they got it. The human rights movement as a distinct, popular social movement swung into gear.[5]

The movement to free Soviet Jewry marks a striking example of Cold War human rights ideology. The movement primarily consisted of Jews in one country seeking the rights of Jews in another country to practice Judaism and to emigrate to Israel. But it presented itself as a claim for the universal human rights to the freedom of conscience and travel. Its target was the Soviet Union. Initially foreign policy realists like Kissinger dismissed the movement; seeking détente, he told President Richard Nixon in no uncertain terms that the United States had no national interest in helping Soviet Jewry, even if they were to be gassed.[6] Eventually, however, the movement managed to ally itself with Cold War strategy. Senator Henry "Scoop" Jackson successfully introduced legislation linking aid to the Soviet Union with the freeing of Soviet Jewish dissidents.[7]

When the Cold War ended, the situation for human rights changed again. For the first time since Nuremberg, where the Americans and the Soviets had cooperated in the aftermath of their World War II alliance, new international tribunals were created to punish terrible wrongs. The international criminal tribunals for Yugoslavia and Rwanda, established in the 1990s, could not have happened during the Cold War, not because there were no massive human rights violations or even genocides during that period, but because every rights violator and genocidal dictator was in the pocket of either the United States or the Soviet Union. With the Soviets no longer on the scene, the United States and Western Europe could use criminal tribunals to make some after-the-fact reparation for their failure to prevent horrible post–Cold War crimes.

As the tribunals were gathering steam, the Western European powers, with guarded U.S. participation, drafted the Rome Treaty, got signatories from around the world, and created the International Criminal Court. This permanent body is supposed to provide a regularized forum for doing the work performed by the special criminal tribunals erected after genocides.[8] The ICC, too, would have been inconceivable during the Cold War, when both superpowers would have worried that such an entity might indict their dictator clients, to their own political detriment.

When the United States invaded Afghanistan and Iraq, its perceived interests regarding international rights enforcement shifted once more. The Clinton administration had signed the Rome Treaty creating the ICC. Under George W. Bush, the United States officially withdrew its signature. In the post-9/11 era, with two wars to fight, Americans worried that their soldiers—or even their civilian leaders—might find themselves charged with war crimes before the ICC.[9]

Beneath the immediate concern with the risks of violating international humanitarian law while war fighting lay a deeper structural reason for the United States to worry about international law. As the dominant global power after the Soviet collapse, the United States could do more or less what it wanted internationally. International law was therefore likely to be used to criticize the United States. Under these circumstances, strengthening the human rights regime more generally might carry appreciable costs to American freedom of action. Giving voice to this view, Secretary of Defense Donald Rumsfeld called international law "a tool of the weak." Scholars complained about "lawfare," the use of human rights law to achieve political or military aims. According to this vision, hampering U.S. freedom to act amounted to abuse of the pure aims of human rights.[10]

To be sure, during this period of war in Afghanistan and Iraq, the overall U.S. position was ambivalence about international law and human rights, not total rejection. In fact, the U.S. government became much more concerned about complying with the laws of war than it had ever been before. Although the executive branch violated international law in Guantánamo, the U.S. Supreme Court, another branch of the government, held that international law had to be applied there, at least insofar as it was incorporated into U.S. domestic law. The Court required hearings for detainees and then struck down the special tribunals that the Bush administration created. International law played a role both times.[11]

Even under George W. Bush, then, the U.S. government never wholly turned its back on the international rights regime—because human rights law still served U.S. interests. Most of the time, under most circumstances, the United States respects human rights much more than most nondemocracies. That respect makes it more legitimate as an international actor, the same way violations make it look illegitimate. For the United States to abandon human rights altogether would take away an important source of international legitimacy. It would provide a long-term advantage to countries that systematically violated or ignored human rights.

The U.S. government, then, has *always* used the ideology of human rights as a political tool, deployed when convenient and ignored otherwise. It allied itself with human rights violators during the Cold War; during the war on terror, it justified its own human rights violations by the necessity of protecting the security of the liberal democratic state. Today, now that the wars in Iraq and Afghanistan have wound down and China has continued to rise, the U.S. interest in focusing on human rights looks much stronger.

The Chen incident showed how far the United States is willing to go, imposing embarrassment and humiliation on China without much concern for the costs to the relationship between the countries. When the United States aligns itself with the international human rights movement in criticizing China, the rights movement will gladly accept its assistance, because China is a far greater rights violator—and because China has not yet accepted the Western universalist conception of human rights that the movement mostly advocates.

Can China Change?

Could all that change? Could China gradually become a human-rights-respecting country, even without becoming a democracy? In the short run, the answer is no. From the Chinese standpoint, the international human rights agenda poses serious dangers, and China can be expected to oppose it. Today, looking at the collapse of the Soviet Union as a negative model, the party believes that lifting its control over speech and protest and many other aspects of Chinese society would likely bring an end to its rule. The party's overarching interest—remaining in power—precludes rapid advances in human rights.

This perspective will also in the near term be expressed in China's international attitude toward other rights violators, who are potential allies. With its increased power, China has increased capacity to block human-rights-related initiatives. Thus, for example, one can safely predict that China would not allow any more ad hoc international tribunals to punish genocidal leaders. The ICC will, for the time being, proceed very slowly and cautiously, concerned not only about the nonassent of the United States but about opposition from China as well.

But this pessimistic vision for the short term is not necessarily stable. In the longer run, China's respect for human rights could evolve—and cool war conditions may encourage that evolution. Begin with the fact that China's stance on human rights is already different from where it was in the early post–Cold War period. In the 1990s, Chinese leaders seemed sympathetic to what Lee Kuan Yew, then prime minister of Singapore, famously called "Asian values," intended as an alternative to what he considered the Western ideals of human rights and democracy. According to this notion, some Western principles of human rights, such as free speech and the value of individual autonomy, were flatly incompatible with "Asian" governance. Lee's argument pitted Western individualism against Asian collectivism. In place of democracy and autonomy, he offered a soft authoritarian regime based on Confucian paternalism.[12]

In contrast, China today typically does not deny that human rights are real or universal. Chinese elites invoke Asian values (or sometimes Confucian values) primarily to justify a development path that ultimately leads toward individualism. Chinese-style Asian values may pass through paternalism as an intermediate stage along the way to individual rights and freedoms. But the end goal is no longer always described in terms so starkly different from the end goals of liberal, rights-respecting democracy. Few of those elites now claim that Chinese values are inevitably collectivist or anti-individualistic.[13]

Instead, when challenged about human rights violations, China's leaders have offered a characteristically pragmatic answer. According to the Chinese government, human rights must be defined so that they include not only negative rights against mistreatment by the government but also positive rights to economic well-being. China's path of party-led economic development, they say, is necessary to create the conditions through which the human rights to health and well-being can be assured. Limitations on the right to free speech or the right of conscience are seen as necessary at this stage and under these conditions.[14]

In essence, the Chinese are saying that granting individual rights of the kind found in Western democracies might well bring

down their system. The system is justified by the fact that it is facilitating rapid economic growth. Therefore, they conclude, China
is not violating human rights when it arrests dissidents and sup-
presses public protest. It is actually doing what it can to realize
other, equally important human rights.

This argument may sound preposterous to Western ears, but it
is worth considering. The claim that human rights include the right
to live decently and well, a right that can only be brought about in
a country with a certain degree of economic development, is one
that some Westerners might accept. Imagine an impoverished person living in a big city in India without access to housing, sewage,
education, or adequate nutrition. He may have the right to free
speech and free exercise of religion. He may even have the right to
vote. But surely this is not sufficient for someone whose life prospects are so extraordinarily limited by circumstance.

Confronting this problem, some philosophers have argued that
human rights should be defined by humans' equal capabilities to
live out the lives they choose for themselves. Living in a place where
there is a certain basic level of economic development is a precon-
dition for being able to exercise other capabilities. According to
this view, economic development is a human right itself, indeed an
important basis for many other human rights.[15]

To be sure, the Chinese government has not fully adopted this
capabilities-centered approach to human rights. But apologists for
the Chinese system are, knowingly or not, offering a variant on it.
They are claiming that freedom from government interference is
meaningful only once the society is rich enough that people can do
something with the rights they have.

Supporters of human rights should not assume that this gradu-
alist argument is intended hypocritically. Many elites in the Communist Party believe sincerely that the system of government they
are pragmatically developing offers the best possible solution to the
improvement of the lives of people in China. It is obviously self-

serving for them to believe that staying in power is necessary for delivering true human rights. But almost all elites everywhere in the world believe that their own influence and power serves the common good—and sometimes they are right.[16]

What all this means is that unlike traditional Chinese communism, with its ideological commitment to reeducation and the creation of a new kind of human being and a new kind of society, China's pragmatic governance today has no principled reason to oppose individual human rights. Indeed, individualism is on the rise in China as a result of party policies promoting entrepreneurship and consumption.

Consumers' Rights

The party's planners want to create a domestic Chinese market capable of buying Chinese goods: in short, they aim to generate a nation of consumers. This kind of consumption in turn requires a culture of individualism in which citizens buy things for themselves instead of just saving for their families and their future. China's emergent cultural individualism will create local demand for greater freedom.

Consumerism, for better or worse, is intimately connected to modern ideas of human rights. Human rights free individuals to pursue life plans in which they experience themselves as making choices. Choices of religion, of belief, and of government fit this description. The right to be treated equally is also necessary to feeling free, and making at least some basic free choices is a minimal condition for dignity.

Citizens who are making free choices in the market will likely want governments to maximize the choices available to them as individuals—and vice versa. Those choices include important life decisions. But they also include the more trivial decisions of everyday existence, decisions that are often expressed in earning a living and buying things with one's money. Production and consumption are important areas for free choice in Western society. It is no coincidence, therefore, that ideas and practices of human rights have arisen in places where economic choice is also relatively unfettered.

While China could develop a culture of consumerism without developing a major demand for human rights, it is far more likely that the gradual increase in consumerism will go hand in hand with greater demand for rights. In general, the two proceed in tandem. Even relatively poor India is strikingly consumerist, in part because of its postcolonial tradition of respecting human rights. Russia developed consumerism at the same time as it was extending individual rights, and although it has since scaled back rights, it has seen no reduction in consumerism. Saudi Arabia, one of a handful of exceptions, has a growing consumer culture without respect for basic individual liberties; yet today there are no examples of countries that have human rights and do not have a consumer culture.[17]

Faced with a gradually increasing demand for rights, the party would increasingly have reason to respect them if it could do so without ceding its governing position. Externally, the benefits of extending human rights within China are real. Respecting rights would make it harder for the West to criticize China. It would remove one of the key American arguments to China's neighbors about why they should fear rising Chinese influence in their region. Internally, responding to a desire for rights could strengthen the party's legitimacy. The all-important question is whether these benefits of increasing respect for rights would outweigh the danger that the party would be weakening its grip on power by loosening its control over Chinese society.

To imagine the possibility of rights-respecting party rule, we need to unsettle our assumption that only democracies respect human rights. Seen historically, authoritarian government and individual liberties have sometimes coexisted. European states, for example, gradually extended rights for a century or more before they adopted democracy.

Over time the party could strengthen the rule of law, move away from arbitrary arrest, expand freedom of religion, and allow more free speech while still maintaining its dominant position and punishing any revolutionary attempt to challenge its power. This vision could follow from the ways the party is now trying to develop a system of governance that solves the problems of democracy without resorting to elections. If the party's legitimacy can be preserved through responsiveness, accountability, and meritocracy, while economic growth proceeds, people might not use their rights to try to undercut the government and establish democracy.

Law to the Rescue?

The possibility that in the long term China may increasingly respect human rights raises a further question for the world more generally: can we imagine international law actually beginning to enforce human rights? At present, the leading human rights treaties provide no provisions for their own enforcement. If a country is found to have violated the rights contained in the treaties, the only cost it suffers is to be deemed outside the community of nations. And if there is one emotion that serial human rights violators tend to lack, it is a sense of shame.

Without ascending into utopianism, it is possible to identify some possible new cool war avenues for the international rights agenda. The key is for advocates to find ways to link rights to economic interests. Today the element of international law that is most consistently enforced is economic law, particularly the law of trade. Where violations of human rights are also violations of international economic agreements, the developing rule of international law could come to affect human rights.

Suppose a country allows local firms to use slave labor. A foreign country could argue before the WTO that this human rights violation is an unfair subsidy of the products being made by slave labor.[18] Or consider a country that tortures its citizens in order to extract oil from some region of the country where the local residents want a larger share of the value created by the oil. Foreign states could claim that the oppression is artificially lowering the costs of oil exports, thereby discriminating against other oil manufacturers.[19]

The exact nature of the claims would vary from case to case. In practice, they would probably be brought to the attention of Western governments by coalitions of human rights activists and corporations whose competitors were benefiting from the abuses, in the way Google tried to challenge China's speech regulations. The strategic goal would be simple: the WTO carries the promise of actual, binding enforcement that nations obey. For the first time, it might be possible to press Western governments to challenge other countries on human rights violations in a venue where a legal victory would have concrete results. If this actually happened, international human rights would look more like law and less like a set of idealistic aspirations.

As always, the real game for human rights advocates is getting friendly governments to exert pressure on the worst violators. For this approach to work, the United States, for example, would have to believe that the benefits of lodging a complaint outweigh its potential costs. The U.S. government has an interest in leveling the playing field for U.S. companies doing business in China. Simultaneously, the United States has an interest in condemning human rights violations in China, both for reasons of principle and in order to gain advantage in the race for allies.

Turning the WTO into a forum where human rights claims could be heard, albeit obliquely, would run the risk of China withdrawing from the treaty. A credible Chinese threat to that effect would likely sink any chance of the WTO regime extending to human rights. But if and when China gradually improves domestic human rights conditions, the benefits it reaps from the WTO may make China more likely to stay and fight than exit the trade regime.

Far less costly would be to argue before a WTO tribunal that the specific practices being criticized have nothing to do with trade discrimination. So long as China adopted this strategy, it could actually become possible for other states to bring trade-linked human rights claims before WTO tribunals.

The deeper point here is that the central positive lesson of the cool war—that economic interdependence can be leveraged to help manage real political conflict—has value for human rights. As we have seen, international law can function and be enforced without a supersovereign so long as the economic interests of the main participants lead them to remain inside the system, even when they lose cases and must pay damages. Indeed, this can occur even when the players, like the United States and China, remain competitors in the arena of global power.

That enforceable international law can coexist with a fundamental struggle among great powers opens the possibility for gradual expansion of the realms in which law operates. The example of human rights suggests that the conditions of cool war need not drive us to despair. To the contrary, there is room for improvement even in the dangerous and complex world in which we now live.

HOW WILL IT END?

The odds are good that in the coming years the China Seas or the Taiwan Strait will see at least one moment of high drama akin to the Cuban missile crisis. In a world of diverging interests and persistent ideological controversy, it will take all the skill of leaders on both sides to keep national pride from driving irrational direct confrontation.

It is also possible that, even consistent with both sides' interests, we will experience shooting wars between U.S. and Chinese allies comparable to the proxy wars of the Cold War. These may well be fights between insurgents and governments, which were common during the Cold War and which remain so today. Already China has supported Bashar al-Assad in Syria while the United States and Europe have, at least indirectly, funneled weapons to Syrian rebels. The West supported the rebels who seceded to form South Sudan while China backed Omar al-Bashir in Khartoum.

The proxy wars could also be between states. If Israel and Iran were to find themselves at war, the United States would support Israel, and China would not want to see Iran totally defeated, at least not while Iran was fighting with missiles and weapons purchased from China. Such a war, which would certainly incorporate Lebanon, would have much in common with the Middle Eastern proxy wars that took place in 1967, 1973, and 1981. A war between North and South Korea might be an even more direct proxy for war between their respective principal allies.

Shooting wars within the cool war need not expand into global conflict, any more than did the insurgent wars in Nicaragua, El Salvador, and Afghanistan or the interstate wars in Korea and Vietnam. In fact, the risks of war spiraling out of control are lower now than during the Cold War. In addition to the difficulty of winning a nuclear war, the United States and China have something very close to mutually assured economic destruction.

Nevertheless, the dangers of war and the potential losses from it are so serious that the world's collective security goal during the cool war years must be to keep the conflict from getting hot if at all possible. The analysis offered in this book leads to several conclusions about how that should be achieved.

First, attempts to manage the cool war must always keep in mind the tremendous gains that both the United States and China have achieved and will continue to experience as a result of economic cooperation. Both sides should use the leverage of their mutually beneficial economic relationship to make fighting less attractive. The positive benefits of trade will not render geopolitical conflict obsolete. But focusing on them can help discourage a too-rapid recourse to violence.

Second, to manage the cool war, it is necessary to focus on how China and the United States are led. We need to understand not only each country's long-term interests but the incentives of the political elites who are in charge. China's Communist Party leadership will want to sustain its position and consolidate its legitimacy without subjecting itself to democratic elections. Any policy initiative must pay close attention to these leaders' motives. The United States and its Western allies must engage the party's interests— without compromising on human rights.

Third, the world is going to change under conditions of cool war, and efforts to keep the war from becoming violent must take account of these changes. New networks of international alliances are emerging. International organizations like the Security Council and the WTO will have more power than before, and should be deployed judiciously and creatively. International economic law can increasingly be enforced as a result of the mutual self-interest of the participants. Global corporations will develop new allegiances as part of a cool war world—but they can also provide incentives to discourage violence and associated economic losses. Human rights, long treated as a rhetorical prop in the struggle between great powers, will still be used as a tool. But over time, respecting rights may come to be in China's interests—with major consequences for the enforcement of human rights everywhere.

What unifies these conclusions is a willingness to embrace persistent contradiction as a fact of our world. We must be prepared to acknowledge both diverging interests and also areas of profound overlap. We must be forthright about ideological distance, yet remain open to the possibility that it can gradually be bridged. We must pay attention to the role of enduring self-interest while also remembering that what we believe our interest to be can change what it actually is.

The United States and China really are opponents—and they really do need each other to prosper. Accepting all this requires changing some of our assumptions about friends and enemies, allies and competitors. It means acknowledging that opposed forces and ideas do not always merge into a grand synthesis, and that their struggle also need not issue in an epic battle to the finish.

Endings

How is the cool war going to end?[1]

The question is as difficult to answer as it is important to ask.

If we knew in advance who was going to win a war, we might not have to fight it at all. If the United States could be certain that China would rise to the status of a comparable or greater superpower, then it might well be foolish to spend political and financial capital to try to impede that rise. If China for its part could be certain that its path to regional and eventually global greatness would effectively be blocked, it would have a reason not to expend vast resources trying to get there.

The fact that the cool war will mostly not be fought through conventional force does not change the nature of this calculus. I have argued that countries' interests have everything to do with their capacities. Geostrategic capacities are measured not in isolation but relative to the capacities of other powers. To predict a period of cool war is therefore to predict that neither side can say with confidence that it *will* win. The fact that each side has good reason to expect that it *can* win is crucial to the expectation that the war will be fought at all.

Nothing could be more uplifting, as the ending to a book like this, than the assertion that peace is logical, that rational people on all sides will avert conflict by acting sensibly. This was the spirit in which Norman Angell concluded *The Great Illusion*. Even the arch-realist Kissinger concluded *On China* in a similar hopeful vein.

But such a conclusion would betray the analysis that I have tried to develop. I have not projected a winner in the cool war— because right now, no one can say who the winner is most likely to be. If violence can be avoided, human well-being improved, and human rights expanded, perhaps everybody could emerge as a winner. If, however, confrontation leads to violence, it is also possible that everyone could lose.

Instead I offer a more modest claim. Geostrategic conflict is inevitable. But mutual economic interdependence can help manage that conflict and keep it from spiraling out of control. And international institutions, much maligned yet also underestimated, are part of the mechanism.

The United States and China are more alike than we tend to believe. Although their interests will continue to diverge, they are gradually growing more similar, not less. If democracy, law, and human rights remain important gaps, China nevertheless has real possibilities to deepen its engagement with many aspects of those values. The cool war will not be over in a generation. But the generation that inherits it will understand its contours much better and can shape the global future with greater confidence and skill.

ACKNOWLEDGMENTS

I would like to thank my colleagues William Alford and Mark Wu for their generosity, comments, conversation, and guidance. The East Asian Legal Studies Program at Harvard Law School and Harvard Center Shanghai provided research support. I am grateful to the numerous Chinese intellectuals who discussed the ideas here with me in Beijing and Shanghai, and who often corrected me or disagreed with me. I want especially to thank my teacher Paul Gewirtz, who first brought me to China, and Julian Gewirtz, who has taught me a great deal about the subject of his expertise. I benefitted from workshop discussions at Graham Allison's Belfer Center for Science and International Affairs, the Weatherhead Center for International Affairs, and the Harvard Law School. I would also like to acknowledge the members of my Fall 2011 course at Harvard Law School, "Cool War: Competition, Cooperation, and the Foundations of International Law," with whom, over the course of a semester, I discussed many of the ideas that eventually made up this book. I am grateful, too, for research assistance from Eli Aizenman, Arielle Davidoff, Yaira Dubin, Alex Triantaphyllis, Alan Rozenshtein, Medha Gargeya, and Caroline Ellison. Hillary Chute read the entire manuscript patiently and closely, and I am deeply thankful to her for this and very much else.

INTRODUCTION

1. For a broad overview of views on this topic, see Edward D. Mansfield and Brian M. Pollins, "Interdependence and Conflict: An Introduction," in *Economic Interdependence and International Conflict: New Perspectives on an Enduring Debate,* ed. Edward D. Mansfield and Brian M. Pollins (Ann Arbor: University of Michigan Press, 2003), 1–28. Mansfield and Pollins emphasize that empirical research has not resolved the debate, since evidence exists to support both sides (4, 8–10). They argue, however, for paying special attention to relevant actors, to the strategic interaction among them, and to "the role played by international economic ties in the processes of conflict generation" (5). To these one might add the institutional frameworks in which the interactions occur.

2. This book thus follows the blueprint laid out by the great Cold War policy-making intellectual George Kennan. In two documents, a secret "long telegram," written for the State Department in 1946, available at http://www.gwu.edu/~nsarchiv/coldwar/documents/episode-1/kennan.htm, and a public essay that he published as "X," "The Sources of Soviet Conduct," *Foreign Affairs* 25, no. 4 (1947): 566–82, Kennan diagnosed the then-new situation of post–World War II geopolitics to frame what would come to be called the Cold War. He offered an influential account of the attitudes and beliefs of the Soviet leadership, one grounded in a clear-eyed understanding of how the Soviet regime held power. And he explained how the United States, in light of its own interests and values, should fight the Cold War while keeping it cold. My conclusion is not to call for a simple theory of containment; but then, properly understood, neither was Kennan's.

3. See the important, jointly produced report by Kenneth Lieberthal and Wang

Jisi, *Addressing U.S.-China Strategic Distrust* (Washington, D.C.: Brookings Institution Press, February 2012), available at http://www.brookings.edu/research/papers/2012/03/30-us-china-lieberthal.

CHAPTER ONE: BOUND TOGETHER

1. René Albrecht-Carrié, *The Concert of Europe* (New York: Walker & Co., 1968), 27.

2. Consider the following statement made by Kurt Campbell, before taking office as Barack Obama's assistant secretary of state for East Asian and Pacific Affairs: "The demands, mostly unanticipated, of the martial campaigns in the Middle East have had the additional consequence of diverting the United States away from the rapidly changing strategic landscape of Asia precisely at a time when China is making enormous strides in military modernization, commercial conquests, diplomatic inroads, and application of soft power. *Rarely in history has a rising power made such prominent gains in the international system largely as a consequence of the actions and inattentiveness of the dominant power.* Indeed, Washington has been mostly unaware of China's gains within the past few years, many of which have come at the expense of the United States" (italics mine). Richard Baum, Kurt M. Campbell, James A. Kelly, and Robert S. Ross, " 'Whither U.S.-China Relations?' Roundtable Discussion," *NBR Analysis* 16 (2005): 25; quoted in Thomas I. Christensen, "Fostering Stability or Creating a Monster?: The Rise of the China and U.S. Policy Toward East Asia," *International Security* 31 (2006): 104.

3. Indeed, by some measures, China has grown by 9.9 percent a year for the past *thirty* years. See Justin Yifu Lin, *Demystifying the Chinese Economy* (Cambridge, U.K.: Cambridge University Press, 2012), 1–2, 222–33.

4. See, for example, OECD Report, "Looking to 2060: Long-term Growth Prospects for the World" (November 2012), which projects that China's economy will pass that of the United States in 2016.

5. Joseph Kahn, "China's Communist Party, 'to Survive,' Opens Its Doors to Capitalists," *New York Times,* November 4, 2002.

6. Myself included. See Noah Feldman, *After Jihad: America and the Struggle for Islamic Democracy* (New York: Farrar, Straus & Giroux, 2003).

7. Overstretch had already been a concern before September 11, 2001. See Paul Kennedy, *The Rise and Fall of the Great Powers: Economic Change and Military Conflict from 1500 to 2000* (New York: Random House, 1987); but the wars in Iraq and Afghanistan were very precise instantiations of the general concern.

8. For a recent account of how this occurred, see Ezra Vogel, *Deng Xiaoping and the Transformation of China* (Cambridge, Mass.: Harvard University Press, 2011).

9. See, for example, statistics compiled by the U.S.-China Business Council, available at https://www.uschina.org/statistics/tradetable.html.

10. For a thorough recent overview, see Wayne M. Morrison, "China-U.S. Trade Issues," Congressional Research Service, RL33536 (2012).

11. See U.S. Treasury, "Major Foreign Holders of Treasury Securities," available

at http://useconomy.about.com/gi/o.htm?zi=1/XJ&zTi=1&sdn=useconomy&cdn =newsissues&tm=15&f=00&tt=11&bt=0&bts=1&zu=http%3A//www.treasury.gov/ resource-center/data-chart-center/tic/Documents/mfh.txt.

12. For aggregate numbers, see Institute of International Education in partnership with the Bureau of Educational and Cultural Affairs, U.S. Department of State, *Open Doors 2012 Report on International Educational Exchange,* available at http:// www.iie.org/Research-and-Publications/Open-Doors. For Chinese students in STEM fields, see Ruth Ellen Wasem, "Immigration of Foreign Nationals with Science, Technology, Engineering, and Mathematics (STEM) Degrees," Congressional Research Service, November 26, 2012, 5, available at http://www.fas.org/sgp/crs/misc/R42530 .pdf.

13. National Bureau of Statistics of China, "Major Figures on Residents from Hong Kong, Macao and Taiwan and Foreigners Covered by 2010 Population Census," available at http://www.stats.gov.cn/english/newsandcomingevents/t20110429_ 402722638.htm.

14. But see Dale C. Copeland, "Trade Expectations and the Outbreak of Peace: Détente 1970–74 and the End of the Cold War 1985–91," in *Power and the Purse: Economic Statecraft, Interdependence, and National Security,* ed. Jean-Marc F. Blanchard, Edward D. Mansfield, and Norrin M. Ripsman (London: Frank Cass, 2000), 15, 25–40. Copeland claims that although trade "remained low throughout the Cold War," détente was nevertheless characterized by increased expectations of future trade, especially on the Soviet side. He then draws direct conclusions for the debate on whether to engage or contain China (57–58).

15. Morrison, "China-U.S. Trade Issues," 29–32, notes that IP-related industries contribute 34.8 percent of the U.S. GDP and that IP enforcement in China remains a major source of concern for U.S. firms.

16. David Hume, "Of the Jealousy of Trade," in *Political Essays,* ed. Knud Haakonsen (Cambridge, U.K.: Cambridge University Press, 1994), 150; and see generally Istvan Hont, *The Jealousy of Trade: International Competition and the Nation-State in Historical Perspective* (Cambridge, Mass.: Harvard University Press, 2005).

17. Originally published as *Europe's Optical Illusion* (London: Simpkin, Marshall, Hamilton, Kent & Co., 1909), it was then expanded and republished as *The Great Illusion* (New York: Cosimo, 2007) (reprint of 1912 edition, n.p.). Under that name, Angell's book went through dozens of printings in the years leading up to 1914. It was translated into twelve languages and widely discussed in the press. It gave its name to the brilliant 1937 antiwar film *Grand Illusion* (*La Grande Illusion*). On Angell's life, see Martin Ceadel, *Living the Great Illusion: Sir Norman Angell, 1872–1967* (Oxford: Oxford University Press, 2009).

18. Liberal internationalists revisited Angell as early as 1971. See Robert Keohane and Joseph Nye, "Transnational Relations and World Politics: Conclusion," *International Organization* 25 (1971): 721, 724. Liberal internationalism is also referred to as "neo-institutionalism" because of its emphasis on institutions; one even hears of "neoliberal institutionalism." The classic contemporary statement is Robert O. Keohane, *After Hegemony: Cooperation and Discord in the World Political Economy*

(Princeton, N.J.: Princeton University Press, 1984). Members of this school typically see international relations in positive-sum terms. See, e.g., Andrew Moravcsik, "Robert Keohane, Political Theorist," in *Power, Interdependence, and Nonstate Actors in World Politics,* ed. Helen V. Milner and Andrew Moravcsik (Princeton, N.J.: Princeton University Press, 2009), 243, 246: "*Stated preferences about the management of world politics are a potentially positive sum variable, rather than a zero-sum constant, as realists had claimed*" (emphasis in original).

Two very useful articles draw distinctions among different types of international relations theorists regarding China; each shows the great complexity of charting various thinkers' positions across the increasingly arcane subcategories of international relations theory. One, Christensen, "Fostering Stability or Creating a Monster?" 81–126, offers a comparison of zero-sum and positive-sum analyses of U.S.-China relations. As Christensen wisely notes, the terms *zero-sum* and *positive-sum* are "ideal types. Almost all relationships in international politics, even the most conflict ridden, fall somewhere along a spectrum between the two" (81n1). As Christensen also points out, as of 2006, there were prominent realists who were optimistic about U.S.-China relations (85).

The other useful article, Aaron L. Friedberg, "The Future of U.S.-China Relations: Is Conflict Inevitable?," *International Security* 30 (2005): 7–45, prefers the categories "optimist" and "pessimist" regarding U.S.-China relations. (These categories were first developed in Aaron L. Friedberg, "Ripe for Rivalry: Prospects for Peace in a Multipolar Asia," *International Security* 18 [1994]: 5–33.) Friedberg's leading categories are "liberal optimists" and "realist pessimists," which correspond very loosely to my categories. But he goes on to explicate the positions of liberal pessimists and realist optimists, not to mention optimists and pessimists of the separate, constructivist school of international relations. There is even a chart (39). Since then, Friedberg has published the excellent *A Contest for Supremacy: China, America, and the Struggle for Mastery in Asia* (New York: W. W. Norton, 2011), wherein he offers a hybrid account ("congagement") of U.S.-China relations. In my own view, optimism and pessimism are not the most useful categories for making sense of the debate, because they do not fully consider the possibility that an American realist might optimistically believe the United States will and can contain China's ambition and defeat it. (An optimistic Chinese realist might think the opposite.)

19. As we shall see, the rise of China has for the first time begun to stir rumblings of an increasingly militarized Japan.

20. See Robert Kagan, *Of Paradise and Power: America and Europe in the New World Order* (New York: Vintage, 2004).

21. Edward N. Luttwak, *The Rise of China vs. the Logic of Strategy* (Cambridge, Mass.: Harvard University Press, 2013). To be sure, Luttwak thinks that China probably will fail to follow its rational interest in adopting military and diplomatic restraint.

22. Scholars of economic interdependence contrast "sensitivity interdependence" with "vulnerability interdependence," depending on what sorts of consequences would be suffered if relations were broken. See David A. Baldwin, "Interdependence

and Power: A Conceptual Analysis," *International Organizations* 34 (1980): 471; see also Edward D. Mansfield and Brian M. Pollins, "Interdependence and Conflict: An Introduction," in *Economic Interdependence and International Conflict: New Perspectives on an Enduring Debate,* ed. Edward D. Mansfield and Brian M. Pollins (Ann Arbor: University of Michigan Press, 2003), 11. The United States and China are in both sorts of relationships. Reduced consumer demand in the United States affects production in China (a classic sensitivity relation); reduced Chinese demand for U.S. bonds would symmetrically affect the United States. Both are also vulnerable to dire consequences if the relationship between the two were to be severed.

23. See, e.g., G. John Ikenberry, "The Rise of China and the Future of the West," *Foreign Affairs* 87 (2008): 23, 26.

24. For a direct comparison between U.S.-China relations and German-British relations before World War I, see Paul A. Papayoanou and Scott L. Kastner, "Sleeping with the (Potential) Enemy: Assessing the U.S. Policy of Engagement with China," in Blanchard, Mansfield, and Ripsman, *Power and the Purse,* 156, 167–72. The authors also consider the relation between Russia and France in the late nineteenth century (165–67). Germany relied on Britain for 20 percent of its "enormous demand for raw materials and foodstuffs," and "Britain was the leading market for German exports" (167–68). The extent of trade between Germany and Britain has been offered as one explanation for why Britain before the war declined to guarantee that it would join France and Russia if they were attacked by Germany; the absence of a guarantee has itself been suggested as a reason why Germany was prepared to go to war. See Paul A. Papayoanou, *Power Ties: Economic Interdependence and War* (Ann Arbor: University of Michigan Press, 1999), 62–87; and Jack S. Levy, "Economic Interdependence, Opportunity Costs, and Peace," in Mansfield and Pollins, eds., *Economic Interdependence and Conflict,* 127, 139.

25. Trade accounted for between 55 and 60 percent of total British national income in the period 1906–13, while trade accounted for 35 to 40 percent of total German national income in the same period. Papayoanou, *Power Ties,* 64. Germany accounted for just over 8 percent of British trade; the United States was between 13 and 15 percent and France around 6 percent. Papayoanou, *Power Ties,* 63.

26. H. C. Allen, *Great Britain and the United States* (New York: St. Martin's Press, 1955), 61–62. On this period, see Aaron L. Friedberg, *The Weary Titan: Britain and the Experience of Relative Decline, 1895–1905* (Princeton, N.J.: Princeton University Press, 1988). See also Bruce Russett, "Violence and Disease: Trade as a Suppressor of Conflict when Suppressors Matter," in Mansfield and Pollins, eds., *Economic Interdependence and Conflict,* 159, 171, noting that "trade and investment ties were very important to the national income" of both Britain and the United States at the time of the power transition between them. See also Bruce Russett, *Community and Contention: Britain and America in the Twentieth Century* (Cambridge, Mass.: MIT Press, 1963).

27. Allen, *Britain and the United States,* 559.

28. The border dispute between Venezuela and British Guiana in 1895, also called the "Venezuela Crisis," marked the one significant point of tension between the

United Kingdom and the United States in this period of American imperial expansion, and it was resolved in favor of U.S. dominance. For a concise textbook overview, see Jerald A. Combs, *The History of American Foreign Policy from 1895,* 4th ed. (New York: M. E. Sharpe, 2012), 9–12.

29. Rudyard Kipling, "The White Man's Burden," *McClure's Magazine,* February 12, 1899. For parallel views of other Britons, see Charles S. Campbell, Jr., *Anglo-American Understanding, 1898–1903* (Baltimore: Johns Hopkins Press, 1957), 25–55. For a recent account of the period in U.S.-U.K. relations, see Kathleen Burk, *Old World, New World: Great Britain and America from the Beginning* (New York: Little, Brown, 2008), 411–36; see also Friedberg, *Weary Titan.*

30. Before the 1930s, central banks mostly held gold and domestic bills of exchange. Between World Wars I and II, central banks sought to achieve greater yields and began to buy short-term British securities. A more precise formulation is harder to reach for reasons of the historical record: until the 1930s, for example, the U.S. Treasury did not keep track of who held U.S. government debt. On the history and rise of sovereign wealth funds, see Lauder Institute of Management and International Studies, University of Pennsylvania, *The Brave New World of Sovereign Wealth Funds* (2010), available at http://knowledge.wharton.upenn.edu/papers/download/052810_Lauder_Sovereign_Wealth_Fund_report_2010.pdf.

CHAPTER TWO: DOOMED TO CONFLICT

1. Chris Wang, "Taiwanese Independence More Popular, Survey Says," *Taipei Times,* August 11, 2012, at http://www.taipeitimes.com/News/taiwan/archives/2012/08/11/2003540007.

2. See the official statement on the website of the Chinese Ministry of Foreign Affairs, "A Policy of 'One Country, Two Systems' on Taiwan," November 17, 2000, available at http://www.fmprc.gov.cn/eng/ziliao/3602/3604/t18027.htm.

3. Scott L. Kastner, *Political Conflict and Economic Interdependence Across the Taiwan Strait and Beyond* (Stanford, Calif.: Stanford University Press, 2009).

4. Henry Kissinger, *On China* (New York: Penguin Press, 2011), 518–21. For the text of the Crowe memorandum, see F.O. 371/257, Eyre Crowe, "Memorandum on the Present State of British Relations with France and Germany," January 1, 2007, in *British Documents on the Origins of the War, Vol. III: The Testing of the Entente 1904–6,* ed. G. P. Gooch and Harold Temperley (London: H.M. Stationery Office, 1928), appendix A, available at http://tmh.floonet.net/pdf/eyre_crowe_memo.pdf.

5. Thucydides, *History of the Peloponnesian War,* 1.23.6.

6. Paul A. Papayoanou, *Power Ties: Economic Interdependence and War* (Ann Arbor: University of Michigan Press, 1999), 78–87.

7. The seminal work for this school of realism is still Kenneth Waltz, *Theory of International Politics* (New York: Random House, 1979). I use the term "realists" to refer to those who are often called "structural realists" or "neorealists"—thinkers who are deeply skeptical of international cooperation because of the anarchic structure of the international order. Many such realists conceptualize international power

struggles as a zero-sum game; and many of those consider U.S.-China relations to be zero-sum. For a leading realist who expresses this zero-sum picture of U.S.-China relations, see John J. Mearsheimer, *The Tragedy of Great Power Politics* (New York: W. W. Norton, 2001), 400ff. See also Joseph M. Grieco, "China and America in the World Polity," in *The Rise of China in Asia,* ed. Carolyn W. Pumphrey (Carlisle Barracks, Pa.: Strategic Studies Institute, 2002), 24–48. It is important to note here that some who consider themselves realists do not accept the view that international relations are always a zero-sum game. See, e.g., Charles L. Glaser, "Realists as Optimists: Cooperation as Self-Help," *International Security* 19 (1995): 50–90.

8. "Preparing for contingencies in the Taiwan Strait remains the principal focus and driver of much of China's military investment. In this context, over the past year, the PLA continued to build the capabilities and develop the doctrine it considers necessary to deter Taiwan from declaring independence; to deter, delay, and deny effective U.S. intervention in a potential cross-Strait conflict; and to defeat Taiwan forces in the event of hostilities." U.S. Department of Defense, *Annual Report to Congress: Military and Security Developments Involving the People's Republic of China 2012,* iv, available at http://s3.documentcloud.org/documents/357540/the-pentagons -assessment-on-chinas-military.pdf.

9. According to one view, China wants to bring Taiwan into its sovereignty but only to avoid Taiwan declaring independence, while the United States wants "only to prevent forceful reunification." See, e.g., Aaron L. Friedberg, "The Future of U.S. China-Relations: Is Conflict Inevitable?," *International Security* 30 (2005): 22. Yet reunification under the background threat of force would have the same geostrategic effect as reunification under force. And at least some Chinese elite actors would clearly value reunification, not just a continued status quo. For a detailed and thoughtful account of the China-Taiwan relationship, see Kastner, *Political Conflict and Economic Interdependence.* On Chinese leaders' goals and tactics, see especially 76–105.

10. For a video of the fall, see http://www.youtube.com/watch?v=dh1N1GIYxDw.

11. For this characterization of liberal hegemony, see G. John Ikenberry, "American Hegemony and East Asian Order," *Australian Journal of International Affairs* 58, no. 3 (2004): 353–67. Ikenberry argues convincingly that the rise of China is likely to lead either to bipolarity in the region or to a gradual abandonment of the region by the United States. The latter seems not to be the course adopted by Barack Obama; the former scenario therefore is presently in play.

12. Kissinger, *On China,* 23–24, 89, 103, 346, 537, 541–42.

13. There is a countervailing cost in that the dollar's exchange rate is also artificially raised, making U.S. exports more costly. Nevertheless the benefit has been estimated at $90 billion a year. See Richard Dobbs et al., *An Exorbitant Privilege? Implications of Reserve Currencies for Competitiveness* (McKinsey Global Institute, December 2009), available at http://www.mckinsey.com/Insights/MGI/Research/ Financial_Markets/An_exorbitant_privilege.

14. On the Sinosphere, see, for example, Joshua A. Fogel, *Articulating the Sinosphere: Sino-Japanese Relations in Space and Time* (Cambridge, Mass.: Harvard University Press, 2009). On the continued vitality of Confucianism—and its changes—see

Daniel A. Bell, *China's New Confucianism: Politics and Everyday Life in a Changing Society* (Princeton, N.J.: Princeton University Press, 2008), especially 3–37. For a strikingly different, neo-Confucian alternative to Bell's left Confucianism, see Yan Xuetong, *Ancient Chinese Thought, Modern Chinese Power* (Princeton, N.J.: Princeton University Press, 2011).

15. Compare Avery Goldstein, *Rising to the Challenge: China's Grand Strategy and International Security* (Stanford, Calif.: Stanford University Press, 2005), 29–40. In my view, the transitional phase for China's grand strategy described by Goldstein (38–39) is essentially over.

16. Graham Allison and Robert Blackwill with Ali Wyne, *Lee Kuan Yew: The Grand Master's Insights on China, the United States, and the World* (Cambridge, Mass.: Belfer Center Studies in International Security, 2013), 2.

17. Kathrin Hille, "China Boosts Defence Spending by 10.7%," *Financial Times,* March 5, 2013. The U.S. Department of Defense estimates China's actual defense spending at between $120 billion and $180 billion. U.S. Department of Defense, *Annual Report to Congress.*

18. Keith Bradsher, "China Is Said to Be Bolstering Missile Capabilities," *New York Times,* August 24, 2012.

19. What is most striking is that most experts in the United States no longer believe space exploration offers significant scientific or technological benefits—which, if true, suggests that in this case, China's main interest is in a kind of anachronistic national prestige better suited to the Cold War era.

20. See, for example, the extended interview with Yan Xuetong published in *Asahi Shimbun,* December 24 and 26, 2012. Yan, the dean of the Institute of Modern International Relations at Tsinghua University and chief editor of the *Chinese Journal of International Politics,* is sometimes perceived as a gadfly, but his views are nevertheless worth noting.

21. Leon E. Panetta, "Remarks by Secretary Panetta on Cybersecurity to the Business Executives for National Security, New York City," October 11, 2012, http://www.defense.gov/transcripts/transcript.aspx?transcriptid=5136.

22. See Jack Goldsmith, "The Significance of Panetta's Cyber Speech and the Persistent Difficulty of Deterring Cyberattacks," available at http://www.lawfareblog.com/2012/10/the-significance-of-panettas-cyber-speech-and-the-persistent-difficulty-of-deterring-cyberattacks/.

23. A report by the U.S. director of national intelligence asserts that "Chinese actors are the world's most active and persistent perpetrators of economic espionage." DNI, Office of the National Counterintelligence Executive, "Foreign Spies Stealing U.S. Economic Secrets in Cyberspace," *Report to Congress on Foreign Economic Collection and Industrial Espionage: 2009–2011* (October 2011).

24. "China and Japan Square Up: The Drums of War," *Economist,* January 19, 2013.

25. See U.S.-China Economic and Security Review Commission, 2011 *Report to Congress* (Washington, D.C.: Government Printing Office, 2011), 180, available at http://www.uscc.gov/annual_report/2011/annual_report_full_11.pdf.

CHAPTER THREE: A ONE-SIDED WAR OF IDEAS

1. Gabriella Blum, *Islands of Agreement: Managing Enduring Armed Rivalries* (Cambridge, Mass.: Harvard University Press, 2007).

2. On the "cat theory," see Ezra Vogel, *Deng Xiaoping and the Transformation of China* (Cambridge, Mass.: Harvard University Press, 2011), 391.

3. Yu Keping, *Democracy Is a Good Thing: Essays on Politics, Society, and Culture in Contemporary China* (Washington, D.C.: Brookings Institution Press, 2009.) Yu's "democracy" is distinct from that of the West and is focused on internal incrementalism. For an analysis of Yu's essay of the same name, see Mark Leonard, *What Does China Think?* (New York: Public Affairs, 2008), 54–60.

4. For the association of democratization with Soviet collapse, see the comments of Chinese intellectual Pan Wei in Leonard, *What Does China Think?*, 61–64.

5. See Kenneth Lieberthal and Wang Jisi, *Addressing U.S.-China Strategic Distrust* (Washington D.C.: Brookings Institution Press, February 2012), available at http://www.brookings.edu/research/papers/2012/03/30-us-china-lieberthal.

6. Paul Kahn, *The Reign of Law:* Marbury v. Madison *and the Construction of America* (New Haven: Yale University Press, 1997).

7. The law professor-activist He Weifang is the most prominent exponent of this view. See He Weifang, *In the Name of Justice: Striving for the Rule of Law in China* (Washington, D.C.: Brookings Institution Press, 2012).

8. For the English text, see "White Paper on Judicial Reform in China," *China Daily,* October 9, 2012, http://www.chinadaily.com.cn/china/2012-10/09/content _15803827.htm. For early analysis, see Carl Minzner, "Chinese Legal Reform: Game On?," *Diplomat,* October 13, 2012.

9. See Minzner, "Chinese Legal Reform," for a comparison with previous years' texts.

10. In a few well-publicized instances, liberals (not revolutionaries) have been able to use the law to improve the conditions of the weak. But they only do so with the consent of the powerful. When the U.S. Supreme Court ruled segregation unconstitutional, this victory for the oppressed was carried out by nine white men, several from the segregated south. They had made a judgment that ending legal segregation would be desirable for the country. Indeed, there is something strange about those with power worrying that law is good for the weak. For centuries, since Proudhon's famous observation that property is theft, radicals and revolutionaries have complained that law serves the powerful, not the disempowered. In reply, those who like law have defended it by saying it is fair and just and that it protects the weak. The idea that law is generally on the side of the oppressed is an apologetic defense of the law against a radical critique. As an account of reality it is sadly lacking. If law were so good for the weak, they wouldn't be weak anymore.

In the international domain, the same situation obtains. See Stephen Holmes, "Why International Justice Limps," *Social Research* 69, no. 4 (2002): 1055–75. Some realists think human rights in particular do not serve the interests of powerful states. Kissinger, for example, often writes as though human rights were a side constraint on real interests, created by the public's quasi-religious (and impliedly irrational) beliefs and principles. Others think human rights are a kind of watered-down utopianism—another secular version of religion. But it would be very surprising if powerful states in Europe—not to mention the United States—had embraced human rights solely on grounds of principle. As Kissinger himself long taught, states have interests, and they tend to act according to their view of what will advance them. And having principles can also be a source of strength for states.

The idealistic view that law can fundamentally transform institutions against the will of those who control them motivates some advocates of international human rights. What is ironic is that it also apparently animates some frightened state actors. In reality, the only way that international human rights can become enforceable internationally is if the powerful agree to make them so.

11. Despite or perhaps because of the 2000 election and subsequent events.

CONCLUSION TO PART ONE: THE CONTRADICTION OF COOL WAR

1. Compare James Fearon, "Rationalist Explanations for War," *International Organization* 49, no. 3 (1995): 379.

CHAPTER FOUR: A GLIMPSE INTO THE NEW CHINA

1. What happened inside the consulate is not known definitively. For two journalistic accounts that draw on interviews, rumor, and anonymous Chinese Internet postings, see FT Edits, *The Bo Xilai Scandal: Power, Death, and Politics in China* (New York: Penguin Portfolio, 2012), and John Garnaut, *The Rise and Fall of the House of Bo: How a Murder Exposed the Cracks in China's Leadership* (New York: Penguin Shorts/Specials, 2012).

2. For an English translation of a firsthand report of the trial, see Donald Clarke, "Unofficial Report of Proceedings in the Gu Kailai Trial," available at http://lawprofessors.typepad.com/china_law_prof_blog/2012/08/unofficial-report-of-proceedings-in-the-gu-kailai-trial.html.

3. Cheng Li, "China's Fifth Generation: Is Diversity a Source of Strength or Weakness?" *Asia Policy* 6 (2008): 53–93, 73, notes that more fifth-generation leaders studied at Beijing University than any other—a change from earlier generations, where Tsinghua dominated. On the cultural importance of the university, see also Jianying Zha, *Tide Players: The Movers and Shakers of a Rising China* (New York: New Press, 2011), 97–137.

4. Elections do occur at lower levels, but candidates are closely vetted and controlled. For a discussion of examples going back to 1980, see Cheng Li, "China's Fifth Generation," 70. For an account of a recent experiment in "inner-party democracy" in Pingchang, Sichuan Province, see Mark Leonard, *What Does China Think?* (New York: Public Affairs, 2008), 51–60.

5. The literature on the production of accountability in China is growing. See, for example, Steve Tsang, "Consultative Leninism: China's New Political Frame-

work?," *Journal of Contemporary China* 18, no. 62 (2009): 865. Tsang emphasizes the party's aim to stay in power; preemptive good governance to avoid democratization; responsiveness to public opinion; pragmatism; and nationalism. See also, in a different vein, Lily L. Tsai, *Accountability without Democracy: Solidary Groups and Public Goods Provision in Rural China* (New York: Cambridge University Press, 2007), which argues that group solidarity based on lineage can function to create solidarity through moral suasion.

CHAPTER FIVE: CHINA'S PERMEABLE ELITE

1. The phrase "people's democratic dictatorship" (*renmin minzhu zhuanzheng*) is occasionally still used, according to Anne-Marie Brady, *Marketing Dictatorship: Propaganda and Thought-Work in Contemporary China* (Plymouth, U.K.: Rowman & Littlefield, 2008), 189. Yet Brady herself writes that the state's legitimacy is based "on popular support rather than moral right" and distinguishes this phrase from the older "dictatorship of the proletariat" (*wuchanjieji zhuanzheng*). As for a better categorization of the system, one recent entrant is "decentralized authoritarianism." See Pierre F. Landry, *Decentralized Authoritarianism in China: The Communist Party's Control of Local Elites in the Post-Mao Era* (New York: Cambridge University Press, 2008); and Chenggang Xu, "The Fundamental Institutions of China's Reforms and Development," *Journal of Economic Literature* 49, no. 4 (2011): 1076, 1082. Xu speaks of "regionally decentralized authoritarianism."

2. For a detailed analysis of the politics of this process, see the five-part series by Cheng Li, "China's Midterm Jockeying: Gearing Up for 2012," *China Leadership Monitor,* available at http://www.brookings.edu/research/papers/2010/02/china-leadership-li.

3. On the patterns of promotion, see most recently Victor Shih, Christopher Adolph, and Mingxing Liu, "Getting Ahead in the Communist Party: Explaining the Advancement of Central Committee Members in China," *American Political Science Review* 106, no. 1 (2012): 166.

4. Family structures are more flexible than is sometimes imagined. Birth is not the only route to kinship. People can marry and create new links where none existed previously. In a pinch, adoption is also possible. Fictive kinship can function as well as the real thing when the situation demands it.

5. Richard McGregor, *The Party: The Secret World of China's Communist Rulers* (New York: Harper, 2010).

6. V. I. Lenin, *What Is to Be Done,* chap. 1.

7. For an account of "left" and "right" among Chinese intellectual elites, see Mark Leonard, *What Does China Think?* (New York: Public Affairs, 2008), 32–50.

8. Indeed, the ancient Athenians actually used lots to select some governmental office holders.

9. Perhaps the oddest—symbolically appropriate even if contextually bizarre— was that Xi had been hit by a thrown chair during a melée at a private meeting with princelings, the so-called red second generation. See Mark Kitto, "What Really

Happened to Xi Jinping," *Prospect,* October 31, 2012, available at http://www
.prospectmagazine.co.uk/blog/xi-jinping-disappearance-truth/.

CHAPTER SIX: LEGITIMACY WITHOUT DEMOCRACY

1. Compare Yuezhi Zhao and Sun Wusan, "Public Opinion Supervision: Possibilities and Limits of the Media in Constraining Local Officials," in *Grassroots Political Reform in Contemporary China*, ed. Elizabeth Perry and Merle Goldman
(Cambridge, Mass.: Harvard University Press, 2007), 300, 321–22; Steve Tsang, "Consultative Leninism: China's New Political Framework?," *Journal of Contemporary
China* 18, no. 62 (2009): 865–80. Party officials use the Internet "as an instrument for
consultation." See also Anne-Marie Brady, *Marketing Dictatorship: Propaganda and
Thought-Work in Contemporary China* (Plymouth, U.K.: Rowman & Littlefield,
2008), 126–45.

2. Jingrong Rong, *Investigative Journalism in China: Journalism, Power, and Society* (New York: Continuum, 2011), 38–48; Benjamin Liebman, "Watchdog or Dema-
gogue? The Media in the Chinese Legal System," *Columbia Law Review* 105 (2005):
1. For an account of how press reforms may have led to Internet speech, see Ya-Wen
Lei, "Institutional-Social Embeddedness of the Public Sphere: Media, Law, Networks,
and the Heterogeneous Development of the Public Sphere in China," unpublished, on
file with the author.

3. Compare Brady, *Marketing Dictatorship,* 128–33.

4. Gary King, Jennifer Pan, and Margaret Roberts, "How Censorship in China
Allows Government Criticism but Silences Collective Expression," *American Political
Science Review* (forthcoming, 2013).

5. See the Pew poll reported in Kaiser Kuo, "Deborah Fallows: Few in China
Complain About Internet Controls" (March 27, 2008), available at http://pewresearch
.org/pubs/776/china-internet.

6. On Home Intelligence, see Ian McLaine, *Ministry of Morale: Home Front
Morale and the Ministry of Information in World War II* (London: Allen & Unwin,
1979); *The British People and World War II: Home Intelligence Reports on Opinion
and Morale, 1940–1944* (Great Britain, Ministry of Information INF 1 .264 & 1 .292),
available at http://images.crl.edu/106.pdf.

7. Estimate for 2011 of 180,000. See more generally Kevin J. O'Brien and Lianji-
ang Li, *Rightful Resistance in Rural China* (Cambridge, U.K.: Cambridge University
Press, 2006).

8. Carl F. Minzner, "Riots and Cover-Ups: Counterproductive Control of Local
Agents in China," *University of Pennsylvania Journal of International Law* 31, no. 1
(2009): 53.

9. According to a 2008 report briefly posted on the website of China's central
bank. See Andrew T. Areddy, "Report: Corrupt Chinese Officials Take $123 Billion
Overseas," *Wall Street Journal China Real Time Report,* June 16, 2011, available at
http://blogs.wsj.com/chinarealtime/2011/06/16/report-corrupt-chinese-officials-take
-123-billion-overseas/.

10. Andrew Wedeman, *Double Paradox: Rapid Growth and Rising Corruption in China* (Ithaca, N.Y.: Cornell University Press, 2012), 111–42.

11. Ibid., 1–14, 177. For an excellent recent review of the voluminous literature on corruption, see Benjamin Olken and Rohini Pande, "Corruption in Developing Countries," *Annual Review of Economics* 4 (2012): 479–509.

12. Wedeman, *Double Paradox,* 142–76; Andrew Wedeman, "Anticorruption Campaigns and the Intensification of Corruption in China," *Journal of Contemporary China* 14, no. 42 (2005).

13. Competition among cities has been seen as a possible explanation for limited urban corruption in other contexts. And see Alberto Ades and Rafael di Tella, "Rents, Competition, and Corruption," *American Economic Review* 89 (1999): 892. For the intensity of regional competition in China and its connection to aspects of China's growth, see Chenggang Xu, "Fundamental Institutions of China's Reforms and Development," *Journal of Economic Literature* 49, no. 4 (2011): 1099–1107.

14. Wedeman, *Double Paradox,* 177–98.

CONCLUSION TO PART TWO: GOVERNANCE AND CONFLICT

1. See Paul A. Papayoanou, *Power Ties: Economic Interdependence and War* (Ann Arbor: University of Michigan Press, 1999), 24–29; and Scott L. Kastner, *Political Conflict and Economic Interdependence Across the Taiwan Strait and Beyond* (Stanford, Calif.: Stanford University Press, 2009), 7–8, 25–29. Both argue that interdependence reduces conflict specifically when political leaders are dependent on internationalist economic interests within their states.

CHAPTER SEVEN: THE RACE FOR ALLIES

1. Yuka Hayashi, "Commander's Rise Shows Japan's Growing Security Role," *Wall Street Journal,* September 13, 2012.

2. Data derived from the WTO Statistics Database, available at http://stat.wto.org/Home/WSDBHome.aspx?Language=.

3. See, for example, Enda Curran, "Asia Leaders Push Regional Trade Pact," *Wall Street Journal,* November 19, 2012, or the essay by Murray Hiebert and Liam Hanlon, "ASEAN and Partners Launch Regional Comprehensive Economic Partnership," for the Center for Strategic and International Studies, available at http://csis.org/publication/asean-and-partners-launch-regional-comprehensive-economic-partnership.

4. U.S. Navy, "Participating Forces," http://www.cpf.navy.mil/rimpac/2012/forces/.

5. David H. Shinn and Joshua Eisenman, *China and Africa: A Century of Engagement* (Philadelphia: University of Pennsylvania Press, 2012), 8–14, offers an overview of differing views of China-Africa relations. See also prominently Deborah Brautigam, *The Dragon's Gift: The Real Story of China in Africa* (New York: Oxford University Press, 2009).

6. See the white paper published by the Chinese government, "China-Africa Economic and Trade Cooperation" (2010), available at http://english.gov.cn/official/2010-12/23/content_1771603.htm. A key phrase used is "the principle of mutual benefit and reciprocity." On China's lack of desire to export its own "development model," see Shinn and Eisenman, *China and Africa*, 4.

7. See Kofi Annan with Nader Mousavizadeh, *Interventions: A Life in War and Peace* (New York: Allen Lane, 2012), 114–19, discussing the responsibility to protect and Annan's 1999 speech calling for a reevaluation of sovereignty to include individual sovereignty alongside national sovereignty.

8. McCain's proposal, delivered in a speech at the Hoover Institution, May 1, 2007, is available at http://media.hoover.org/sites/default/files/documents/McCain_05-01-07.pdf.

9. One account of the dynamics of this mechanism may be drawn from the classic Albert O. Hirschman, *National Power and the Structure of Foreign Trade* (Berkeley: University of California Press, 1945, 1980); for an elaboration, see Rawi Abdelal and Jonathan Kirshner, "Strategy, Economic Relations, and the Definition of National Interests," in *Power and the Purse: Economic Statecraft, Interdependence, and National Security,* ed. Jean-Marc F. Blanchard, Edward D. Mansfield, and Norrin M. Ripsman, 119, 120–21. On this view, participation in a free-trade agreement will shift the smaller participating state's perception of its own interest so that "it will converge toward that of the larger." The reason is that the free-trade agreement will provide an advantage to those actors within the smaller state who are most closely aligned with the larger state. They will then form coalitions to advance those interests. See also David Singh Grewal, *Network Power: The Social Dynamics of Globalization* (New Haven, Conn.: Yale University Press, 2009).

CHAPTER EIGHT: MANAGING WAR, BUILDING PEACE

1. Immanuel Kant, "Perpetual Peace: A Philosophical Sketch," in *Political Writings,* ed. Hans Reiss (Cambridge, U.K.: Cambridge University Press, 1970), 93.

2. The date was October 5, 1795 (13 Vendémiaire Year 4 of the revolutionary calendar).

3. Thomas Hobbes, *Leviathan,* ed. Richard Tuck (Cambridge, U.K.: Cambridge University Press, 1996), 90 (chap. 14).

4. This describes roughly the events in a real case: *Japan-Taxes on Alcoholic Beverages,* Panel Reports I and II and Appellate Body Report, available at https://docs.wto.org/dol2fe/Pages/FE_Search/FE_S_S006.aspx?Query=(@Symbol=%20wt/ds8/*)&Language=ENGLISH&Context=FomerScriptedSearch&languageUIChanged=true#.

5. Thus far sanctions have been permitted for costs incurred only after the panel reached its decision, not retroactively. This has led to a discussion of a so-called remedy gap, since countries can in theory cheat the system by taking advantage of the gains of discriminatory trade practices and then stopping them before any damages are incurred. See, e.g., Rachel Brewster, "The Remedy Gap: Institutional Design, Re-

taliation, and Trade Law Enforcement," *The George Washington Law Review* 80, no. 1 (2011): 102. According to the legal rules, however, damages could in principle be imposed for harms done before the panel's judgment was reached. I owe this latter observation to Mark Wu.

6. Compare Dale C. Copeland, "Trade Expectations and the Outbreak of Peace: Détente 1970–74 and the End of the Cold War 1985–91," in *Power and the Purse: Economic Statecraft, Interdependence, and National Security*, ed. Jean-Marc F. Blanchard, Edward D. Mansfield, and Norrin M. Ripsman (London: Frank Cass, 2000), 15: "If trade expectations are positive, dependent states will expect to realize the positive benefits of trade into the future, and thus be more inclined toward peace." Copeland is writing about peace rather than compliance with the trade regime, but his core point about future expectations of trade is transferable.

7. Mark Wu, "Free Trade and the Protection of Public Morals," *Yale Journal of International Law* 33 (2008): 215–51.

8. See Liu Ting, "CUEB Delegation Won the 2nd Prize for the First China WTO Moot Court Competition," available at Capital University of Economics and Business, http://english.cueb.edu.cn/News/latest_news/24721.htm.

9. Ibid.

10. Anthea Roberts, "Clash of Paradigms: Actors and Analogies Shaping the Investment Treaty System," *American Journal of International Law* 106 (2012).

11. It is possible for countries—like people—to make unenforceable agreements that are more like nonbinding promises than true guarantees. Reputational harm could be the only consequence of failing to comply. Eventually the country that was not trusted by others would find it difficult to cooperate with anyone. But promises that cannot be enforced are less useful than promises that can be. The signatories to treaties may want something closer to a contract—one that may be enforceable with actual consequences.

CHAPTER NINE: CORPORATE COOL WAR

1. James Glanz and John Markoff, "Vast Hacking by a China Fearful of the Web," *New York Times,* December 4, 2010. The cables were part of the Wikileaks cache. For an academic overview, see Cynthia Liu, "Internet Censorship as a Trade Barrier: A Look at the WTO Consistency of the Great Firewall in the Wake of the China-Google Dispute," *Georgetown Journal of International Law* 42, no. 4 (2011): 1199–1240.

2. Google also issued a white paper fleshing out its argument, "Enabling Trade in the Era of Information Technologies: Breaking Down Barriers to the Free Flow of Information," available at http://static.googleusercontent.com/external_content/untrusted_dlcp/www.google.com/en/us/googleblogs/pdfs/trade_free_flow_of_information.pdf.

3. See, for example, "Bashing Baidu: State Television Fires on China's Google," *Economist*, April 27, 2011. There is a state-owned entrant in to the search market, called Jike, but it did not yet exist when the Google events took place in 2010.

4. Ibid.

5. François Xavier d'Entrecolles. See William T. Rowe, *China's Last Empire: The Great Qing* (Cambridge, Mass.: Harvard University Press, 2009), 84.

6. For an account of China's incentives in acquitting oil firms, see, for example, Ilan Alon and Aleh Cherp, "Is China's Outward Investment in Oil a Global Security Concern?," *Columbia FDI Perspectives,* no. 81, October 22, 2012.

7. "CNOOC Withdraws Unocal Bid," Xinhua News Agency, August 3, 2005, available at http://www.china.org.cn/english/2005/Aug/137165.htm. Unocal later sold to Chevron for $18.4 billion, just a bit below the CNOOC offer: "Chevron Nabs Unocal," *Petroleum News,* April 10, 2005, at http://www.petroleumnews.com/pntruncate/25987919.shtml.

CHAPTER TEN: THE FUTURE OF HUMAN RIGHTS

1. Legal writers contrast international humanitarian law, which applies without exception in wars, with human rights law, the regime that applies in peacetime (and sometimes allows temporary exceptions). In ordinary discourse, the rights guaranteed by international humanitarian law are considered a species of human rights; I follow this assumption here.

2. Noah Feldman, *Scorpions: The Battle and Triumphs of FDR's Great Supreme Court Justices* (New York: Twelve, 2010), 276–80.

3. Samuel Moyn, *The Last Utopia* (Cambridge, Mass.: Harvard University Press, 2010), 3.

4. G. B. Trudeau, *Doonesbury's Greatest Hits* (New York: Holt, Rinehart & Winston, 1978).

5. Moyn, *Last Utopia,* 121.

6. Clyde Haberman, "Decades Later, Kissinger's Words Stir Fresh Outrage Among Jews," *New York Times,* December 16, 2010.

7. Gal Beckerman, *When They Come for Us, We'll be Gone: The Epic Struggle to Save Soviet Jewry* (New York: Mariner Books, 2011).

8. The ICC so far has opened just seven investigations, all focused on Africa. In the case of Sudanese president Omar al-Bashir, the ICC has made the first steps toward holding a sitting leader responsible for his actions by charging him with genocide and crimes against humanity. But the ICC has its limits. It focuses on the worst humanitarian law violations: genocide, crimes against humanity, war crimes, and international aggression. It has no jurisdiction, however, over ordinary restrictions on individual rights, such as whether a country gives its inhabitants free speech. If it did, it probably would never have gained the requisite number of signatures to come into force.

9. Lee Feinstein and Tod Lindberg, *Means to an End* (Washington, D.C.: Brookings Institution Press, 2009), 47. The Senate had not voted to approve the treaty for ratification.

10. Jack Landman Goldsmith, "The Self-Defeating International Criminal Court," *University of Chicago Law Review* 70 (2003): 89.

11. In *Hamdi v. Rumsfeld*, 542 U.S. 507 (2004), 548–52, the case that specified due process rights for war-on-terror detainees, Justice David Souter in his concurrence explained that the government could not claim to be detaining Hamdi under the laws of war since it had apparently violated the Geneva Conventions in holding him incommunicado without a hearing. In *Hamdan v. Rumsfeld*, 548 U.S. 557 (2006), Justice John Paul Stevens for the Court held that the Geneva Conventions applied to Guantánamo detainees and that the Uniform Code of Military Justice incorporates the conventions' requirement that detainees be tried in tribunals with the same rules as courts martial.

12. For a discussion, see Michael A. Barr, "Lee Kuan Yew and the 'Asian Values' Debate," *Asian Studies Review* 24, no. 3 (2000): 309–34. See also Joshua Cooper Ramo's interview with Lee Kuan Yew appended to Ramo, "The Beijing Consensus," available at http://www.politicalchina.org/uploadfile/200909/20090918021638239 .pdf.

13. Thus, the official National Human Rights Action Plan of China (2012–2015), released June 6, 2012, available at http://news.xinhuanet.com/english/china/2012-06/ 11/c_131645029.htm, puts it this way: "Taking all types of human rights as interdependent and inseparable, the Chinese government determines to promote the coordinated development of economic, social and cultural rights as well as civil and political rights, and the balanced development of *individual and collective* human rights" (emphasis added).

14. The National Human Rights Action Plan expressly articulates what it calls "the principle of pursuing practicality" as follows: "The Chinese government respects the principle of universality of human rights, but also upholds proceeding from China's national conditions and new realities to advance the development of its human rights cause on a practical basis." The plan further states that "it should be remembered that China remains a developing country that is fraught with problems from unbalanced, uncoordinated and unsustainable development. Due to the influences and limitations of natural, historical and cultural factors, as well as the current level of economic and social development, China still confronts many challenges in the development of its human rights cause and it has a long way to go before it attains the lofty goal of full enjoyment of human rights." Nevertheless, the report claims, "the Chinese government has unswervingly combined safeguarding human rights with promoting scientific development and social harmony, kept improving its institutional arrangements for ensuring and improving its people's livelihood, vigorously boosted employment, speeded up the development of various social undertakings, promoted equal access to basic public services, gradually improved a social security system that covers both urban and rural areas, initially established a basic medical care and health service system benefiting both urban and rural residents, strived to develop cultural and educational undertakings, and effectively guaranteed the rights of all members of society to equal participation and development."

15. Amartya Sen, *Inequality Reexamined* (Cambridge, Mass.: Harvard University Press, 1992); Martha C. Nussbaum and Amartya Sen, eds., *The Quality of Life* (Oxford: Clarendon Press, 1993); Martha Nussbaum, "Capabilities as Fundamental

Entitlements: Sen and Social Justice," *Feminist Economics* 9 (2003): 33–59; and Amartya Sen, "Human Rights and Capabilities," *Journal of Human Development* 6, no. 2 (2005): 151–66.

16. The Chinese Communist Party's version of human rights treats human rights as a means to accomplishing a goal, rather than as an end in itself. Yet some Westerners are willing to imagine the temporary violation of certain rights under limited conditions, like torturing a suspected terrorist to find the location of a ticking time bomb.

17. On India's growing consumerism, see, for example, Reeba Zachariah, "D-Street Looks for New Growth Leaders in Consumerist India," *Times of India*, March 14, 2011, available at http://articles.timesofindia.indiatimes.com/2011-03-14/india-business/28688054_1_public-issues-jubilant-foodworks-listing-price; Zachariah describes public offerings of shares in firms devoted to the domestic Indian consumer market. See also Leela Fernandes, "The Political Economy of Lifestyle: Consumption, India's Middle Class, and State-Led Development," in *The New Middle Classes: Globalizing Lifestyles, Consumerism and Environmental Concern,* ed. Hellmuth Lange and Lars Meier (London: Springer, 2009), 219.

18. Under the GATT, there was a "morality exception" to allow countries to discriminate against others who, for example, engaged in the slave trade. See Steve Charnovitz, "The Moral Exception in Trade Policy," 38 *Virginia Journal of International Law* 689 (1998). But what I am describing runs in the opposite direction: accusing a country of trade discrimination because it enslaves people.

19. International investment treaties, like trade treaties, typically require a government to treat foreign firms equitably. So similar arguments could be deployed using the ICSID regime. Of course, human rights claims can also be used the opposite way, to justify regulations that disadvantage foreign investor firms. See Luke Eric Peterson, *Human Rights and Bilateral Investment Treaties: Mapping the Role of Human Rights Law within Investor-State Arbitration* (Montreal, Que.: Rights and Democracy, 2009).

CONCLUSION: HOW WILL IT END?

1. I owe this formulation to Jaemin Feldman.

INDEX

China (cont.)
  Tiananmen uprising, 38, 59, 61, 90,
    92
  Tibet and, 90, 110
  trade and, xiii, 6, 7, 11–13, 15, 17, 49,
    98, 102, 103–4, 105, 124, 132, 133,
    160
  U.S. and economic incentives to avoid
    conflict, 15, 17, 163–64
  U.S. as adversary, xii
  U.S. as debtor, xii, 6, 11–12
  U.S. as strategic opponent, 48
  U.S. as trading partner, xii, xiii, 6, 7,
    12–13, 15, 34, 49, 102
  U.S. business investment in, 6
  U.S. consulate in Chengdu, 55,
    178n 1
  U.S cultural interactions with, 6
  U.S. military strength and policy of
    containment, xii–xiii, 20–25,
    104–5, 110, 129, 170n 2
  U.S. relations with, 14, 15, 171n 18
  U.S. war, realism and the case for
    conflict, 17–19, 129
  U.S. war, Taiwan scenario and,
    16–17, 20–25, 175n 8, 175n 9
  Wenzhou train crash, 86–88
  WTO and, 123–24, 140–41, 183n 9
China Natural Offshore Oil Company
  (CNOOC)
  bid for U.S. oil company Unocal,
    142–43
  takeover bid for Canadian energy
    firm Nexen, 143–44
Chinese Communist Party, xii, xiii–xiv,
  95–96
  businesses, oversight and protection
    of and as revenue, 133–35, 139
  capitalism and, 4, 5, 57
  Central Discipline Commission, 95
  citizen protests and, 92, 156
  communism and, xiii, 4, 5, 37, 39,
    42, 64, 78, 81, 157
  Communist Youth League, 80

conservatives (the left) in, 60, 66, 76,
  81, 179n 7
consumer society as goal of, 157–59
control of China's economy and, 4
corruption in, 65, 92–96, 181n 13
as "decentralized authoritarianism,"
  179n 1
"eight immortals," 57
fifth generation of leaders, 59, 178n 3
government accountability and, xiv,
  69, 178n 5
incentives for cooperation with the
  U.S., 129–30
interests of, economic growth and, 98
interests of, precluding advances in
  human rights, 154–57, 163
internal divisions, xiv, 80–82
legitimacy of, xiv, 86–96, 97, 179n 1
Lenin's design for, 78–79
meritocracy and, 66, 68, 80–82, 83,
  97
military policies, 23–25, 129
nationalism to justify governing,
  32–33
new model of governance, 65–70, 96,
  97–98
nomenklatura system, 79, 96
as permeable elite, 78–80
Politburo, 57, 72, 83
Politburo Standing Committee,
  60–61, 66, 72, 83, 131
pragmatism and, xiii–xiv, 37–39, 108,
  116, 155, 157, 178n 5
"princelings," 57–58, 64, 65, 66,
  80–82, 83, 179n 4
public discourse on Bo Xilai scandal,
  67
public discourse via weibo and, 88
rejection of Maoism, 37
response to dissidents, 90–91
revolution and, 79
right-wing of, 81, 179n 7
rise of Bo Xilai as illustrative of new
  China, 57–61

ABOUT THE AUTHOR

NOAH FELDMAN is Bemis Professor of International Law at Harvard University and the author of five previous books, most recently *Scorpions: The Battles and Triumphs of FDR's Great Supreme Court Justices* (2011). A Senior Fellow of the Society of Fellows at Harvard, Feldman has a bachelor's degree from Harvard, a law degree from Yale, and a doctorate in Islamic thought from Oxford, where he was a Rhodes Scholar. He clerked for Justice David Souter on the Supreme Court. In 2003, he served as senior constitutional advisor to the Coalition Provisional Authority in Iraq, and subsequently advised members of the Iraqi Governing Council on the drafting of an interim constitution. He has been a contributing writer for *The New York Times Magazine* and is columnist for Bloomberg View.

ABOUT THE TYPE

This book was set in Sabon, a typeface designed by the well-known German typographer Jan Tschichold (1902-74). Sabon's design is based on the original letterforms of Claude Garamond and was created specifically to be used for three sources: foundry type for hand composition, Linotype, and Monotype. Tschichold named his typeface for the famous Frankfurt typefounder Jacques Sabon, who died in 1580.